Pagan Portals

Spellcraft and Spellwork

A Guide to the Magical Practice of Spells

What people are saying about

Spellcraft and Spellwork

Finally, in a modern market perhaps over-saturated with esoteric titles that seek to impress the reader in some way, a book with an authentic voice, which, far from seeking to impress the reader, inspires them to read and take each piece of advice to nurture their practice.

Spellcraft and Spellwork: A Guide to the Magical Practice of Spells is an excellent introduction to understanding the basics of magic and spellcasting, how to cast all kinds of spells, and the work behind it, from the definition of types of magic to the creation and use of each spell for your own empowering.

Ariana Carrasca is naturally eloquent, disciplined in her teaching, and patient with the reader, guiding them through each step of spellwork and practice. This book will be pivotal in training and teaching many new followers and seekers of the Craft.

Elhoim Leafar, tarotist, dowser, author of *Dream Witchery: Folk Magic, Recipes & Spells from South America for Witches & Brujas*

This is not your typical spell book. Here you will not find mindless magical directions and impersonal correspondences; rather the tools to create your own. Insightful, sensitive, and tremendously well researched; Ariana Carrasca guides you through the intrinsically personal experience that is spell craft. This is a must read for deepening the "why" behind the "how" in the realm of magic.

Hannah Hawthorn, creator of *Simply Witched* and author of *The Magick of Birthdays: Rituals, Spells and Recipes for Honouring your Solar Return*

This book gifts to the reader a grounded, accessible, and in-depth overview into the very foundation of magical practice. With hands-on exercises which will aid those dipping their toes into spellcraft with the tools required to craft and curate their own magical workings, as well as invaluable information regarding the theory, history, and background of magic. Ariana Carrasca's voice guides you, like a kind and generous teacher, through the often difficult to navigate landscape of magic and spellwork with passion and empowerment. A perfect primer, introduction, or even refresher for the modern-day magical practitioner!

Mhara Starling, author of *Welsh Witchcraft: A Guide to the Spirits, Lore and Magic of Wales*

Pagan Portals

Spellcraft and Spellwork

A Guide to the Magical Practice of Spells

Ariana Carrasca,
The Oak Witch

MOON
BOOKS
London, UK
Washington, DC, USA

CollectiveInk

First published by Moon Books, 2024
Moon Books is an imprint of Collective Ink Ltd.,
Unit 11, Shepperton House, 89 Shepperton Road, London, N1 3DF
office@collectiveinkbooks.com
www.collectiveinkbooks.com
www.moon-books.net

For distributor details and how to order please visit the 'Ordering' section on our website.

Text copyright: Ariana Carrasca 2023

ISBN: 978 1 80341 253 5
978 1 80341 254 2 (ebook)
Library of Congress Control Number: 2023936096

A CIP catalogue record for this book is available from the British Library.

Design: Lapiz Digital Services

Printed and bound by CPI Group (UK) Ltd, Croydon, CR0 4YY
Printed in North America by CPI GPS partners

We operate a distinctive and ethical publishing philosophy in
all areas of our business, from our global network of authors to
production and worldwide distribution.

Contents

Introduction

Deep within each of us there exists the fantastical world of spells, witches and wizards; where images of bubbling cauldrons, waving wands and pointy hats aren't too unfamiliar. But how far from reality is all of this? Misconceptions of witchcraft and the practice of (occult) magic have often painted spells as either an action of a wicked evil character or a device to make the impossible possible. Magic can indeed be used to harm others, and it can make amazing things happen for us, but the reality is spell practice is much more accessible than many think.

Spellcasting is a deeply personal, practical and spiritual way to help make things happen in our lives, and spells as a term itself is a massively broad term for a praxis incorporating many different methodologies. It can encompass the movement of energy, connecting with spirits, feeding into your inner power and ultimately, transforming your goals into reality through real work. There are boundless types of spells, ways to perform them, ways that they work, results that they provide, and it can take some time for one to wrap their head around it all.

Though spells are a defining feature of witchcraft as a magical practice, it is not solely witches that perform them. Folk magic practitioners, ceremonial magicians and many other types of magical workers can all utilise spellwork in their practices for a variety of reasons, as we all have our own reasons and ways to do magic. A spell can be as detailed as an elaborate ritual with Latin incantations and spirit conjurations, or as simple as a single lit tealight candle and quiet concentration. Many magic workers look to ancient tomes and grimoires as a source of knowledge for their spellwork, whereas many others can be more intuitive in their approach; styling a spell around more modern themes that surround their everyday life. You could be reconstructing a phylactery from the Greek Magical Papyri or stirring some positive energy into your morning cup of tea, both are spells in their own right and can be deeply powerful. Charm bags, poppets, anointed candles, herb-filled jars, strings tied with numerous knots – whatever your spell looks like, whether you prefer the simplicity or the intricate detail, if it helps you get the magic done then that's what matters most.

There are countless factors that can vary the individual's experience of their spellwork process, including your theological approach. Take, for example, those more inclined towards an animistic view of the world; despite being a broad term with many definitions, animists generally see the world and all its inhabitants as having a spirit or some form of spirit essence and may connect with plants as spirit allies to assist them in their magical working. On the other hand, those who are more strictly polytheist may prefer to call upon specific deities they venerate to help the magic flow towards the desired goal. Some people work exclusively with the concept of energy to power and push forward the magic, whilst others have a strong bond with a familiar spirit to help them as well. Each approach is valid and can work just as well for an individual, the trick is finding what approach works best for you.

What lies true for all spells is that its function is largely attempting to achieve a desired goal and enact that change through a series of actions. Many aspects of the process can influence the success of your spell, such as the strength of your will, how focused your mind is and the symbology of the accompanying tools towards your initial goal. What tools you need for your spells is up to you and can vary with what you are trying to achieve. Spellcraft and spellwork is ultimately, quite a subjective experience, it's your decision what you decide to include in your spells. There are magic workers that only utilise their mind in their spells and others that use whatever the natural world provides them. That is the beauty of magic and spells, it's truly an intrinsically personal experience that we curate ourselves.

Usually, the first exposure many magic workers have to spells are the ones detailed in big spell encyclopaedia books, which has a danger of fostering a more impersonal approach when looking to begin working spells. Whilst performing other practitioner's spells is not an issue and can work just as well, the best way to enter your magical practice is understanding how to come to terms with the tools you need to create your own spell. Our magical practices are our own paths, not anybody else's, and they should be personalised to our own preferences. We all have our own unique creative flavour to bring to this world, and that should be highlighted in our spells.

This book aims to take the reader through both the inner and outer processes of spellcrafting and spellworking, to help practitioners build on their spellcasting skills and perform magic that can transform their life. Through understanding baseline magical and spell theory, the spellcaster will be able to take confident steps in their practice and shape their magic so that it is more authentic and individual to the practitioner. This book will detail such theory and help the magic worker apply it in praxis. Questions will be answered that many might be too afraid to ask, such as, how does one come up with a good spell intention? Or how do you know what to put in a spell? When would you need to cast spells and what do you do with it when it's done? It is hoped that the reader is left with the knowledge and skills to help them go into their magical workings with ease and confidence.

Chapter 1

An Insight into the History of Magic

Magic. It is truly an enigmatic, ancient force. Perhaps that sounds a little superfluous, but it's true. Magic is amazing. Since humans have lived and connected to their environment, the practice of magic has captivated many. People saw magic and spirits all around them, from rivers and forests as deities, phenomena like the howling wind as terrible and terrific spirits, mountains as the bodies of giants and many more wonders. Possibly one of the most fascinating traces of magical history we have are sacred sites that were constructed to map astronomical observations. One notable example is Stonehenge in Wiltshire, which was seemingly constructed with the summer solstice sunrise aligned through the two entrance stones.[1] It was a place of ritualistic pilgrimage and is a tradition continued into the modern day, where many people travel to the stones on the solstices and equinoxes to magically celebrate the changing seasons. The survival of these ritual monuments is an insight into how spiritually connecting to the landscape in a physical manner was important to ancient peoples and has carried on overtime.

It is not just the changing seasons and planetary movements that was of great importance either, dating back centuries, people across all early civilisations on this Earth have held close relationships with the Otherworld and utilised hidden forces to obtain their desires, ensure their survival or follow a path of spiritual ascension. We can look to Animism as an early example of all of these things. It is an ideology which – depending on your strict definition – generally perceives that the natural world, objects, places, and even natural phenomena, as all being inhabited by a spirit or some form of spiritual essence; every tangible being has an intangible being within. It is a worldview that is regarded to be the oldest religion, though the term itself was coined by Edward Burnett Tylor in 1871.[2] The idea that there exists something else amongst us, outside of our physical perception, is inherently magical. Have you ever stood in the middle of a forest, listening to the wind swaying the trees and rustling the leaves, and just felt that there is something else out there? Animism is a little bit like that, that feeling of otherness beyond what we normally perceive in the material world. In the modern age, many have abandoned this philosophy, but animism still exists in many spiritual cultures and religious faiths, especially paganism and the occult.

Divination is another magical practice that has had a strong presence amongst civilisations since antiquity, with the Mesopotamians, Egyptians, Iranians, Greeks, Etruscans and Romans all forming their own divinatory systems which varied geographically.[3] Seemingly, part of what sets humans apart from other fauna species on this Earth is the ability to introspect, intuit and be aware of ourselves, our surroundings and how it affects us. We attempt to make sense of it all through various means, but one of which has often been divination, seeking answers from outside of us to make the path ahead of us clearer. While Tarot (cartomancy) is a clear favourite amongst modern spiritually inclined people, cleromancy is one which features in many ancient sources, involving the casting of lots, thought to have originated in ancient Egypt. In modern day, it does still persist, with casting of runes being a favourite method for deity communication for many Heathens. Divination serves as a way to navigate the unknown, something which will always have a strong presence amongst us and develops as time does.

As writing technology developed, so did the accessibility of magic. The development of writing technology was highly influential on the democratisation of magic and general esoterica.

As early as 5th-4th century BC, we can see the very first written incantations on Mesopotamian clay tablets,[4] and as the methods by which people were able to record and write their knowledge improved, books of magic evolved, and magic practitioners began collating their occult knowledge in tomes called grimoires. One of the earliest grimoires is thought to be the Testament of Solomon compiled in the 1st century CE, if we're excluding the Greek Magical Papyri (PGM) which whilst its contents date to 30 BCE – 390 CE, it was actually made into a book in 1928 and 1931. As time went on, these magical texts became much more accessible, and as more people became literate, these grimoires were translated to various languages in tandem with printing becoming more common and commercialised. The knowledge of magic was spreading and reaching more people, and as it did, magic itself evolved and transformed. Of course, magic exists outside of books and is a lived experience. There exist numerous survived cultures that orally passed down their spiritual wisdom, or what some would class as magic. This indeed is just as enriched as magic that has been written down throughout the ages, especially in regard to practices closed through hereditary lineages or initiations.

A large majority of what modern witchcraft consists of stems from European histories of witchcraft, and in particular, British witchcraft. Looking at British magical history, we can see how magico-medicinal practitioners called the cunning folk had access to grimoires and would employ rituals and spells from them for their clients and use the texts in the creation of their written charms. This grimoire occult magic blended in easily to the everyday folk customs of the cunning person, and this happened all across Europe, magical practices evolving with the ability to expand their magical reading and written knowledge. Even when illiterate, some cunning folk would possess grimoires regardless to impress their clientele and make it seem as though they held more arcane knowledge or prowess than they actually owned. This can also give us an insight into how vastly perceptions of magic have changed and evolved over time too. Influential grimoires in pre-reformation England included the *Sworn Book of Honorius*, *Ars Notoria*, the *Key of Solomon*, *Three Books of Occult Philosophy*, the *Discoverie of Witchcraft* and very many more.[5]

Grimoires are a further example of ancient magic that has been revived in the modern day, with pagans and magical practitioners across the globe creating their own grimoires, more commonly referred to as "Book of Shadows". This term is often credited to Gerald Gardner from his book of ritual and magic called *The Gardnerian Book of Shadows*, which has served as a foundation for many Initiatory Wiccan traditions. However, Doreen Valiente (one of Gardner's High Priestesses and highly influential in the modern witchcraft movement) states that Gardner rather took the term from a magazine called *The Occult Observer* from 1949, where an article called "The Book of Shadows" by a then well-known palmist called Mir Bashir wrote about an ancient Sanskrit manuscript.[6] Nowadays, Book of Shadows as a term has become the normal name for a personal book of magic, rituals and spells.

Though indeed Gardner is not free from criticism, we must acknowledge the influence he had on magical history. We can attribute the popularity of the modern witchcraft movement to many figures in Wiccan history. Wicca itself is an amalgamation of various occult influences that interested Gardner, especially the writings of Margaret Murray and Hermetic Order of the Golden Dawn, which in turn is descended from traditions such as Rosicrucianism, Theosophy, Freemasonry, and much more. Gardner's Wicca was catalysed by the repeal of the Witchcraft and Vagrancy Act in 1951, which let magical practitioners be able to practice more openly and freely, without fear of persecution.[7]

Gardner thus released his books on witchcraft, as did many of his initiates, such as Valiente. Some of Gardner's initiates then branched off and formed their own lineages and traditions, and this is where we began to see the spread of modern witchcraft and ritual across the world, for example, with Raymond Buckland bringing Wicca over to the United States.

So, Gardner's Wicca certainly had its impact and still does to this day. Whilst countless other magical traditions outside of witchcraft have its own rich history, one cannot deny witchcraft's iconic history. Especially as we consider all the different types of witchcraft that evolved off of Wicca's success. Traditional Witchcraft is often seen as an example of this, as it was birthed by the rise in witches and magical practitioners who did not feel called to Gardner's ways and wanted to differentiate their craft. Where Wicca focuses a more ceremonial western occult flavour, Traditional Witchcraft narrows down on a folk magic approach, centred closely amongst the practitioner's bioregional landscape. In more recent years, to the authors observation, there has been a boom in what is referred to as "folk witchcraft," which does not necessarily follow a structure like Wicca or Traditional Witchcraft does that often relies on a duotheistic, binary approach to divinity. Rather, it simplifies witchcraft to an animistic lens, heavily concentrated on folk magical practices as a core part of the path.

Looking forward into the modern day, it is evident that magic has made its presence in the digital world, of which was certainly clear during the COVID 19 pandemic and rise in internet witchcraft. Magical communities online are flourishing, and knowledge of magic is more accessible than ever before (for better or for worse). People can share their magical ideas and practices, relate to each other's experiences and debate about magical theory with others from all around the world. One debate that is frequently held in online spaces is the differentiation of magic and magick. It seemed as though, as communities of magical practitioners evolved, a need for establishing magic as a genuine, esoteric concept was needed and many began adopting the spelling "magick" rather than magic as a way to establish this. This spelling is commonly attributed to British occultist Aleister Crowley, who people say added on the 'k' to differentiating magic as a spiritual practice from that of stage magicians, illusionists or fantasy. Whilst this may be true,[8] Crowley himself specifically writes in his work *Magic in Theory and Practice* that he didn't want the 'undesirable connotations' that come with terms from particular traditions such as Theosophy and Spiritualism,[9] that were popular at the time. This rather implies that Crowley wanted his understanding of magic to be distinct from other spiritual understandings of magic. Going further, others posit that Crowley created the spelling; however, the truth is that he simply repopularised it. The spelling of "magick" can be seen in some of the early grimoires, such as Henry Cornelius Agrippa's *Three Books of Occult Philosophy*, which dates back to 1531. The simplest answer to the question is to use whichever spelling you prefer best, as the experience magic is not something that can be limited to a single world anyway.

A previously outlined, magic is an experience. It can be a study, a journal, but ultimately it is a quest. Whatever path you travel down to journey the quest is your choice. As we can see in the modern day, the practice of magic and ancient ways of approaching theism is having a revival; from the countless pagan and polytheistic traditions (be it Heathenry, Celtic paths, Hellenism or Roman paganism, Rodnovery, etc.), to Wicca and its subgroups based on lineages (Gardnerian or Alexandrian, etc.), to Traditional Witchcraft and its many branching paths (Chumbley's Sabbatic Craft, Cochrane's Clan of Tubal Cain, the Feri tradition and many others) and further to Western Esoteric traditions such as Thelema. These things are rarely ever created in a vacuum and many of these traditions are formed from being influenced by what came before. With the fact that so many of these paths have strong, flourishing communities both offline and online, it's evident that a growing number of people are feeling the call of magic.

Chapter 2

Magical Theory

Definitions of Magic

We have seen how magic has fascinated people for centuries but pinning down exactly what is happening when we witness the power of magic has puzzled many. Magical practitioners, witches, occultists and the like have all attempted to find a clear definition for magic, yet we're still to find a single all-encompassing definition that satisfies all.

Arguably the most famous and often quoted definition has to be from British occultist and 'wickedest man in the world'[1] Aleister Crowley, who stated that magic is "the Science and Art of causing Change to occur in conformity with Will".[2] To Crowley, "Every intentional act is a Magickal Act",[3] therefore, any spiritual and mundane action that leads the individual towards achieving their *True Will* is "magick". Crowley's teachings gave birth to the ceremonial tradition of Thelema and in his idea of what magic is, we can understand it as the art of applying knowledge of yourself and your conditions in action. Our *True Will* is our ultimate purpose, and every action we take should work towards our Will. This definition of magic outlines the nature of magic well, in that magic is ambiguously both a science and an art. We can measure our outcomes and perfect a spell recipe, for example, but magic is also an artform. It is a highly subjective experience, open to interpretation by whomever is looking upon it and something which cannot by singularly identified. It flows with the individual. Though something to be said for Crowley's definition is how it is contingent upon this idea of one's *True Will*, which can miss out on other perspectives such as those from folk practitioners.

There have been countless people since Crowley who have made their own adjustments to his definition, more notably Dion Fortune is said to have altered it to "Magick is the art of causing changes in consciousness in conformity with Will".[4] Alternatively, Donald Michael Kraig in his work *Modern Magick* expanded upon Crowley's definition with: "Magick is the science and art of causing change (in consciousness) to occur in conformity with will, using means not currently understood by traditional Western science".[5] It's interesting here that Kraig chose to define magic directly in relation to its inability to be explained by mundane science; potentially highlighting the cryptic nature of magic may give those unbeknownst to the world of the occult a better understanding of how we approach the employment of magic.

However, in my opinion, the most convincing adaption to Crowley's definition is from Jason Miller in his work *The Elements of Spellcrafting*, where magic is the "Science and Art of influencing change to occur in conformity with Will".[6] The distinction of magic being something which influences change, as opposed to outwardly causing it, is genius. By identifying that magic is rather influential, that it increases the likelihood of a particular action or behaviour happening, helps put in perspective of the reality of what magic can and cannot do.

How many times has the dear reader had to explain to someone outside of the magical community that magic is not what it is like in films? That we do not turn people into toads just for fun, or that we can't make them win the lottery? If we see magic as an influence, we know that we can employ prosperity magic to increase our chances of a stronger income or sudden windfall of money, as opposed to a guaranteed successful draw in the lottery. Its more about influencing the odds or turning factors in our favour, as opposed to guaranteeing you an immediate result of whatever you wish for. It is no doubt that magic has made things happen for many which would otherwise seem

13

impossible, but that just lends itself to the ambiguous nature of magic. One last definition of magic which calls to the puzzling yet wonderful disposition of magic is from Harry Josephine Giles' essay "Altars of Transition", in the book *The Modern Craft*.[7] Though their definition of magic was in context to their gender transition journey, it is a beautiful way of describing magic, where it is "the doing without knowing, the becoming without being, the spiritual practice of hope."

It is clear that many have various ideas of what magic is and how it works, and that is because it is an intensely individual experience. We all have our own perspectives based on our personal experiences, and that is the beauty of magic. Our differences don't need to be contradictions, and the fact that we cannot agree on a singular definition is what makes magic so powerful.

Models of Magic

Though we may not have a universal definition of magic, we do have some frameworks of how it works. Several models of magic have been established by practitioners in order to explain the fundamental beliefs behind the functionality of magic. Understanding these different models can be incredibly useful in building a magical practice and advancing your spellwork. When we know how something works, we can put it to use more efficiently.

Starting with **the spirit model**, which is arguably the oldest model of magic we have record of. This model posits that there is an Otherworld beyond our physical plane that is inhabited with all sorts of different types of autonomous spiritual entities. Such spirits can include angels, demons, deities, land spirits, plant spirits, the fair folk, etc. When we perform magic through the spirit model, we understand that the works are carried out and function through the help of entities enlisted in the magical process. Behind the scenes these spirits are able to control, manipulate and influence situations in a spiritual plane we don't readily have access to, so that they align and fulfil the magical goal.

There are countless methods one may use to reach out to spirits. Ceremonial traditions look to grimoires and utilise spirit conjuration rituals detailed in those tomes to connect to spirits. Of course, praying is an obvious example, often falsely considered to be solely a Christian practice. We can pray to a particular spirit, maybe our deities or ancestors, to help us in a certain situation and give us some guidance. Prayer can follow a traditional format depending on a particular religious tradition, or it can be completely intuitive. In many folk magical traditions, praying to or petitioning saints is a common way to work magic using the spirit model, and sub-methods of saint spirit work can depend on cultural perspective. Working with a familiar spirit is an additionally common practice for many folk traditions and practices of witchcraft, with a familiar spirit simply entailing forming a close bond with a particular spirit.

A popular method of spirit communication within folk and traditional witchcraft paths is the use of spirit flight. This is a practice involving a trance-induced, ecstatic, visionary experience, where your spirit leaves your corporeal being and "flies" to the Otherworld. By utilising breathwork, rapid or rhythmic movements and sometimes magical tools such as a stang or flying ointment, we can enter these altered states of consciousness to allow our spirit to enter a different realm. A realm where we abandon our material bindings and let our spirit be free, to welcome the magical and connect to spirits. If spirit flight as a skill is harnessed well enough, once the person "crosses the hedge", they can call upon their desired spirit and ask them to help make their magic work.

The next most common model of magic is referred to as **the energy model**. The underline premise of this model is that reality is comprised of energy. Energy is everywhere and every action or phenomena in the world is a sequence of energetic movements. As magical practitioners, we employ techniques to manipulate and move that energy towards a desired goal and that serves the fundamental process for how magical workings, such as spells, work. Here, there is no need to enlist the help of spirits to do the work for us, as we do it ourselves. Though, it's important to note that the spirit and energy model are not mutually exclusive, and many magical practitioners work both models in their path very intuitively and fluidly.

To give an example, many witches incorporate plants in their spells. It's a practice which reflects the cunning folk and their use of herbs in their magical and medicinal practices, as well as an ode to herbalism. With the energy model, we connect to the plants' energy to power the spell, but one may also connect to the spirit of the plant, asking the plant to assist us in the magical working. The energy of a particular plant (or object and such) is not too dissimilar to a human's personality. Plants can have numerous energetic associations (personality traits), as we do. Sometimes we come across somebody that has a particular "vibe" about them or that they give off a certain type of energy. You can feel the energy shift in the room when there's been an argument. This model is about tapping into those movements and making magic with them.

The psychological model is a further semi-popular model in today's witchcraft and magical communities. Sigmund Freud's psychodynamic theories revolutionised psychology and has since influenced many schools of thought on how the mind works and explanations for human behaviour. The psychological approach to magic is underlined by this, and posits that the unconscious can be tapped into in order to affect change, through subliminal symbolism and altered states of consciousness. In this case, intentional magical action is training your unconscious mind to influence changes in your life.

The psychological approach can also entail explaining the way magic works through what is known as the placebo effect. With this model, it is being aware of magic that is not necessarily mystical or occult-ish, but rather the mind tricking itself into making something work. There are unnumerable studies into the placebo effect, with it producing extraordinary results. Ultimately with this model, its less about magic being a spiritual experience, and more about rather something that works, so why question it?

An example of a practice that relies heavily on this psychological foundation is the use of sigil magic. Occultist and artist, Austin Osman Spare was, one of the first to pioneer the concept of sigils in magic and his ideas were very impactful for Western occultism. Sigils are where any wish or goal is made into a symbol, and this would be established into your subconscious, with you being consciously aware of said process. Sigils as a magical method have developed a lot since Spare, with many modern witches taking a more artistic and intuitive approach and less formulaic.

By no means is this an exhaustive summary of all the models of magic, however, these are simply a few of the most present models seen in various popular traditions and paths of paganism, witchcraft and occultism. What is important to acknowledge when identifying with different models of magic and understanding your own magical philosophy, is the concept of gnosis. Gnosis can be understood as the idea of spiritual truths and is often divided into three terms, UPG, SPG and VPG. Unverified Personal Gnosis (UPG) is likely more familiar to many, as it is usually employed in a casual context to refer to one's own personal unique experience or own opinion. To further explain using polytheistic framework, many people feel called to work with deities in their magical path and have spiritual experiences with them. Deities can be highly enigmatic, and the experiences with them can be very ambiguous, where deities can appear to us in different ways. One practitioner may see a particular deity as helpful in one regard, whereas another may experience the opposite. This is where UPG comes into play, where it identifies that we have a particular magical or spiritual truth that is "true" for us, but not necessarily for everybody else. Anyone who has also had this gnosis experience independently to you, is then called Shared Personal Gnosis (SPG). Verified Personal Gnosis (VPG) is the idea of gnosis revealed to you independently is later validated by a primary source of some kind. Though these terms are more often than not used in a pagan context, they can and do get it further applied to magical practice. For example, you may believe a certain spell works a certain way because it's your UPG.

Exercise 1 – Establishing Your Magical Worldview
This is rather a loaded question, but how do you see the world? From the models of magic that we've already outlined, and perhaps doing further research on others, how do you reason the world of magic? Here are some questions to get you thinking:

• What is the natural world to you? Is it just all just exactly how we see it as in the physical plane? Do you think there's something us as humans can't readily see?
• Do you believe in spirits? Do you believe in deities? Where do you think these spirits came from? What do you think these spirits do? Why do they need or want our offerings? Why do you think they help us?

- Do you believe in the spiritual concept of energy? How different do you think it is to the scientific concept of energy? Do you think they can co-exist well?
- How much of magic do you think is confirmation bias? Do you there is a clear line between the mundane and the magical? Do you believe that magic is mainly works through the placebo effect?

Think deeply on these models, asking yourself why and why again. This may take days, months, and you may not produce a single answer, or any answer. There is no right or wrong here, simply just who you are. But reflecting on a model and working within specific ones can be helpful when authenticating your craft and strengthening your magic.

Principles of Magic

Theoretical analyses on why magic works have been proposed all throughout the history of magic. These principles of magic, also known as metaphysical laws, act as rules that magic follows, but not rules that every magical practitioner must follow. Magic is fluid, and many different traditions have formed as a result of certain principles across different cultures. Understanding the principles of magic can make for a stronger application of magic in one's own practice, as when you can confidently comprehend what is happening metaphysically when you are enacting magic, then curating your spell will be just that little bit easier. What follows is not an extensive list, but simply a few of the main principles commonly discussed.

The law of knowledge is a fairly simple concept, that understanding brings control. What is often said in many magical paths is that there is a lot of studying and research. There is a lot of truth to this, as knowledge is power, and more contextual information to a practice, ourselves or magic, can bring about new understandings of our own power and make our own magic more effective. This law can be paired with the ancient Greek maxim "Know Thyself", initially found inscribed in the Temple of Apollo at Delphi, followed by "Nothing to Excess" and "Certainty Brings Insanity". The better we can truly know ourselves, our mind, body and spirit, and how these three aspects interconnect and influence our behaviour and existence, the better our magic will be as we have more control. This idea of knowing ourselves is a fluid, ever-growing process. We are not static – we are always changing, learning, bettering ourselves. It is through the law of knowledge that we recognise this and continue to apply it.

The law of knowledge is put into practice quite easily. Beyond putting it into practice through journeying to understand ourselves better, we can also see it in the context of soaking up knowledge and information of different kinds; learning as much as we can of cultural, historical and general background contexts of what we do. In spells, this can include learning about correspondences before we utilise them, or understanding why certain cultures gave specific deities specific offerings.

This brings us to a further principle of magic, **the law of correspondence**. The term 'correspondence' was coined by the scientist and mystic Emanuel Swedenborg, and in his 1757 work *Heaven and Hell*, he describes how the "whole natural world corresponds to the spiritual world".[8] Swedenborg's ideas expanded beyond this, but his revelation of correspondences went on to be highly influential in the occult world, developing into the law of correspondence. This law presents the notion that there is a relationship between two distinct planes of existence: the natural plane and the spiritual plane, and these planes are interconnected. The Hermetic phrase 'as above, so below' is often explained utilising Swedenborg's concept of correspondence, outlining how the macrocosm is reflected in the microcosm and vice versa.

Correspondences are fundamental to the occult and general esoterica. We utilise these correspondences in all manners of magical workings, and they are a core aspect of how we craft together spells and charms. Planetary magic is a prime example of the law of correspondence in action, where we invoke the planetary energy to feel the influence of the planet's powers in our lives. If a person wants to develop their self-love, they may invoke Venusian energy into their lives, as Venus corresponds with love and beauty. As above (the planet Venus and its energy of love and beauty), so below, (increased feelings of love and beauty within ourselves or about ourselves).

The law of similarity is a principle of magic we see written in James George Frazer's 1890 work *The Golden Bough*, where he coined the term "sympathetic magic", to describe this law and the law of contagion (discussed below). The law of similarity is the idea that if there is a symmetrical quality between two concepts, then we can establish a magical connection. In more easy-to-understand terms, like produces like or an effect resembles its cause.

To give an example of this principle of magic in action, we can look to the folk magical use of poppets. A poppet is a type of spell where the magical practitioner constructs a figure to resemble the target that they wish to perform magic on. The common misconception is that this magical craft is exclusive to traditions of Hoodoo or Vodun and is innately baneful in nature, but neither of these notions are true. The use of poppets can be seen across many different folk magical traditions, and you can use poppets for any type of magic, not solely for magic that harmful in nature. With a poppet, the law of similarity is utilised in the construction of the figure resembling your target, as like produces like.

In the same body of work, James George Frazer describes **the law of contagion** to be where things have been in contact with each other, they can further continue to magically interact once separated. Even across long distances, once the physical contact has been severed, they can act on one another, hence why this principle is also known as the "law of contact".

Running with the poppet example, the law of contagion would be what you stuff the poppet with. Usually, a poppet is stuffed with a taglock, otherwise known as a link, which is the idea that you have an object you include has both a physical and metaphysical link to your target. To link your poppet back to your target, one may place the nail clippings or hair of the target into the poppet. Those personal materials were once a part of the target's body, which have now been separated, but still are metaphysically connected to the individual. Therefore, when it is put into the poppet, which through sympathetic magic resembles the target already, these two laws work in tandem to achieve the goal of the spell.

Taglocks from a human can be anything you deem appropriate, but what is commonly used is hair, nail clippings and bodily fluids. Taglocks which are also utilised are things like photographs, the target's full name and date of birth, astrological natal chart, and any other personal information directly linked to that individual. These perhaps don't necessarily follow the law of contagion in the traditional sense they haven't been physically connected to that individual and then separated, but they are certainly symbolically connected to the person.

Chapter 3

Practical Magic

In theory, there are countless types of magic. Anything that involves human behaviour and the desire to seek change or influence a situation, magic can be involved.

To understand its function better, people have identified labels of what magic is and it especially helps people define what magical practices they specialise in. When connecting with other magical practitioners, labels can allow us to better understand what the other person's practice is like. So, labels certainly have their uses, but at times they can put us in a box and they can be a hindrance in how we rely on them. Sometimes a label is not enough to encapsulate the nuances behind how the magic works and the individual experiences of that type of magic. Labels can dumb down a magical practice and oversimplify what is inherently complex. Nevertheless, we can look at what types of magic there are, and the different magical workings people utilise in practical magic to strengthen our baseline understandings of the functionality of spells.

Spectrums of Practical Magic

We can first outline the spectrums of which magic occurs. People define the practice of magic in binary concepts a lot of the time, where there are two types of magic that contrast each other. The reality is that these dichotomic labels are more like a spectrum, where the contrasting magics can interact and often reflect each other. Binary understandings of magic and the divine can limit the potential these phenomena hold, and whilst there isn't anything necessarily wrong with using binary terms, it's worth understanding that these spiritual experiences and concepts exist way beyond our human language can even comprehend.

The first spectrum of magic to discuss is **folk magic and ceremonial magic**. These terms are two understandings of magic and its general format in practice. Other labels for folk and ceremonial magic are also commonly implemented, such as thaumaturgy and theurgy, low and high magic and active and passive magic respectively.

Folk magic encompasses a down-to-earth, practical type of magic, used to solve or influence more common, day-to-day problems and situations. Historically, it is magic for the common folk, for the people, by the people. It is an active type of magic that seeks to improve more practice or mundane aspects of our lives, aesthetically involving everyday objects and hands-on crafting. The concept of folk magic is not a singular thing, and there is no such thing as a monolithic folk magic tradition. The style and flavour of folk magic, what it looks like in theory and practice, will differ from culture to culture and many countries and cultures have their own labels for what folk magic is and for who practices it. Historically in England, there are numerous names for varying folk medicinal-magical practitioners including toad doctors, charmers, pellars, the cunning folk or wise women/wise men and more.

Ceremonial magic, on the other hand, deals with more ritualistic, methodical magic that aims to approach divinity in some way; whether that be to elevate the individual towards the divine, or to become divine (apotheosis), for example. This type of magic brings the practitioner to higher states of consciousness and tends to be more spiritual in nature, rather than practical like folk magic. Ceremonial magic is often defined by longer, elaborate rituals, symbolic use of tools such as a sword or athame, incantations and much more. Traditions of ceremonial magic has formed over the years, from Thelema to Qabalah,[1] Enochian magic, Demonology and more.

Another common false dichotomy expressed in discussions of magic is the idea of **baneful magic versus beneficial magic**. Further labels have been synonymised to these categories, one popular example being black magic and white magic. In both academic and practitioner spaces, these terms are found widespread, but many advise to not utilise them and favour more inclusive language. This is due to the racist connotations they have predominantly stemmed from the United States, where the magical and religious practices of Hoodoo and Vodun are seen stereotyped as "black magic", which is further identified as "evil", which is reductionist and a false generalisation. Other parallel labels include positive and negative magic and light and dark magic.

Baneful magic involves magic designed to intentionally inflict harm, whereas beneficial magic is utilised to heal or benefit oneself or others. The former is judged as 'bad', whilst the latter is 'good', which are often quite arbitrary statements. Magic is simply magic. It is a tool; tools can be used for a multitude of purposes and are not defined by moral qualities. A hammer used to build something is not referred to as a "good hammer", nor is one used for destruction labelled a "bad hammer". Going even further into this analogy, using hammers destructively can lead to good outcomes. Sometimes you need to tear down something to make way for something better. Should we be placing inherent markers of goodness and badness onto certain magics? Baneful magic can be seen as a righteous decision in some cases, for example, cursing an abuser who escaped the criminal justice system or hexing fascist political figures, regimes or parties. Beneficial magic can be seen as ethically questionable in certain circumstances, such as attracting a new lover by making them fall in love with you; this can be seen as very manipulative and controlling, and directly infringes on the person's autonomy. The goal here is not to make any definitive rules about how one should employ their magic, but rather aims to highlight how magical practitioners often live in the "grey". The structure in which we employ magic is a spectrum and its down to the individual to decide how they shall utilise it.

Magical Intentions

Often practitioners use labels associated with the intention or goal by which they are utilising the magic. There are countless of ways one may wish to employ magic, but as far as most common types of magic in accordance with its intention or goal, these are some of the main ones discussed.

Protection magic is a favourite amongst many, mostly due to the fact that it is so important. Magic can be employed to protect, defend against or ward off any unwanted disruptive energy, spirits, objects, phenomena or people. There is an array of various protective practices one can use, from wards, to amulets, to return to sender spells; people have been coming up with ways to protect themselves from the unknown for hundreds of years.

As discussed before, **baneful magic** is magic that is utilised to harm. Curses, hexes, jinxes, casting the evil eye at somebody, and even some forms of love magic or domination spells are all examples of baneful magic. Any magical working that harmfully disrupts somebody's autonomy and is outwardly making their life worse in a particular way, could be classified as baneful magic.

Humans love, love. As such, many love, **love magic** too, and it is such a broad category of magic. One would immediately jump to spells designed to attract a new partner to your life, or bring your ex back, but love magic can also include self-love, familial love and strengthening friendships. Self-care, improving your mental health or even acts of forgiveness or apologising, can all be aspects of self-love and in turn, love magic too.

Throughout history, communities of people have relied on **healing magic** to help them survive through illness, unexplainable disease, health conditions or any trouble they deal with. Modern scientific medicine has improved so much that the majority of us no longer have to rely on magic, however, many of us still do. That is not to say that we cannot take a dual approach whereby we implement professional treatment alongside some magical help. Healing magic may include utilising magic to aid in recovery, to banish an illness or to ease symptoms.

Prosperity magic is another practitioner favourite as we navigate this increasingly capitalist and consumerist world. The need to support oneself and ensure stability in finances is something that is pressing for a lot of people on this Earth, and as such, spirituality has always held space for prosperity and abundance. One only needs to look at the many folk customs around the world that prevent the loss of money or ensure riches. A Chinese custom includes always being sure to close the lid of the toilet when you flush, so your money doesn't flush with it, and to give another example, in Russia, if you whistle inside your home, it means you're whistling away all of your money. Magic involving prosperity can entail increasing money or income, job hunting, increasing resources or improving assets or skills.

Justice magic is a type of magic that is important for perhaps less self-centred reasons. A lot of the magical practitioners in history have always been outcasts, on the fringes of society, marginalised. We live in a world which is rather cruel, and many Western societies are built upon the outcomes of slavery, oppression, colonisation and more. We have systematic structures that benefit from the disadvantage of minority groups and sometimes we can't just leave it to systemic justice, especially with the rise in fascism in political structures and abhorrent crimes of the police. There have been numerous times in history where practitioners have employed magic to fight a cause; Dion Fortune was said to have guided others to focus on visualisations to repel Nazis, as well as Gardner's account of witches from the New Forest Coven performing a ritual to ward off Hitler from the invasion of Britain.[2] Magic is powerful and empowers the people who need it most and we can use it to fight back, to right wrongs and enforce change.

Types of Practical Magic

Magic can be found in all things, and we can see this when identifying the different types of magic in practice. Starting with **planetary magic**, which involves any magical working done in accordance with the seven classical planets. These are the two luminaries; the Sun and Moon (of course, not technically planets in today's modern scientific understanding), Mars, Mercury, Venus, Saturn and Jupiter. Planetary magic can look like invoking any of these planetary energies to feel their influence in our lives, working with any deities or spirits associated with the planets, creating sigils with planetary magic squares (kameas) or crafting planetary talismans or amulets. Each of the seven days of the week further correspond to a particular planet, so one can work with these planetary energies day by day.

Looking more closely with working with the Moon, we have **lunar magic**, which often refers to a magical practitioner aligning their magic to the phases of the moon. It follows basic astronomy, where we have the New Moon (symbolising new beginnings), the waxing phases (Waxing Crescent, First Quarter and Waxing Gibbous; all symbolising growth and manifesting a goal in action), the Full Moon (where we harvest out efforts and reap the reward), and the waning phases (Waning Gibbous, Last Quarter and Waning Crescent; where we rest and reflect). To put it more simply, the waxing phases align with attracting and bringing things into our lives, whereas the waning phases are for banishing and removing what we don't want or no longer need. The New Moon is often referred to as the dark moon, and both here and at the Full Moon, do we find magical practitioners reserving divination and bigger magics for these times of the month.

Solar magic, on the other hand, is any magic that involves working with the Sun. This can include simple folk practices such as charging objects with the energy of the Sun (as many do with the Full Moon too) or acknowledging the solar festivals that take place throughout the year, such as the equinoxes and solstices. The Winter Solstice (20–23 Dec) symbolises the rebirth of the Sun, the Spring Equinox (21–22 March) is a symbol of new life and new beginnings, the Summer Solstice (20–23 June) is a celebration of abundance and manifestation, and the Autumn Equinox (20–23 September) is a festival of thanksgiving, harvest and reflection. Many people mark these days in the astronomical calendar and make a point to celebrate them, as they are a symbol of the changing seasons. Other festivals have been noted as a part of a neopagan "Wheel of the Year", with names having been attributed to ancient Gaelic Celtic festivals, such as Bealtaine (Beltane, 30 April – 1 May) and Lúnasa (Lammas, 31 July – 1 August).[3]

The elements are a strong feature of numerous magical traditions, and **elemental magic** is the term often associated with this. The elements here most commonly refer to the five elements seen in western occultism (Earth, Air, Fire, Water and Spirit). The elements are all around us, working intricately together and elemental magic highlights the role each individual element plays. Air magic involves working magic with the element air, so this may look like working with incantations, sound cleansings, the use of incense or movement and dancing. Earth magic is rather broad and encompasses magic involving aspects of the earth; plants, trees, mushrooms, stones, bones, the soil of the Earth itself etc. Fire magic is often simpler, with any magical workings involving the use of fire, usually candle spells or cauldron fires. Water magic involves magical workings utilising water, whether it be cleansings, floor washes, water scrying, etc. Spirit magic is more spiritual in nature, working on our magical selves, relationship with the divine and such.

Diving further into earth magic, **plant magic** is magic that incorporated the use of herbs, flowers, trees, but also other natural material such as roots, fungi, even bryophytes and grasses, etc. Each plant can have various corresponding magical attributes that can vary from person to person, according to their UPG, culture and tradition.

Crystal magic is any magic that involves crystals, or rather, minerals. Minerals are a solid chemical substance that are naturally formed and can develop through a variety of geologically processes. They are the constituents of almost everything on our Earth, but when a chemical substance structure repeats, a crystal is formed. Crystals as a term within modern spirituality refers to crystal structures of minerals, that are often artificially enhanced for the mass market.[4] Crystal magic posits that each crystal/mineral has an inherent spiritual quality, often associated with some form of healing which is a practice grown out of new age spirituality.

Natural magic is a term for magic that involves working directly with the natural world, often juxtaposing with ceremonial spirit work. This is rather broad and can encompass within the term elemental magic, solar and lunar magic, planetary magic, plant magic and more.

Kitchen magic (or mostly known as kitchen witchcraft) is the use of the kitchen in any magical practice. This can constitute of cooking or baking in spells, or generally any form of food or drink preparation with magical intent behind it. **Hearth magic** is very similar to this and involves the same type of magic, but also includes other types of homemade preparations (perhaps such as magical soaps and other toiletries) and cleaning (floor washes, types of cleansings, etc.). It is essentially magic done in the hearth, the home.

Colour magic is another simpler idea, where it refers to the corresponding magical symbolism behind each colour. Colour correspondences can massively vary from culture to culture and based upon individual preference (as with most, if not all, correspondences). Red can symbolise danger, precaution and warning here in western areas such as the UK or United States, whereas in eastern countries such as China, it is a very lucky colour. People in the US see green as a colour relating to wealth, perhaps where their money is green, but here in the UK, our money is not entirely green per say, so that same reasoning behind the correspondence does not relate to us. Colour magic in practice can be very easy, such as intentionally wearing a colour whose magical properties you would like to invite in your day or choosing spell ingredients with a particular colour to correspond that intention, using a black candle for protection, in a protection spell, for example.

Number magic (referred to largely as numerology) is the symbology of numbers, seen in a lot of occult practices and in divinatory systems such as tarot or playing card cartomancy. Each number has a spiritual value, one (or ace) symbolising new beginnings, two – relationships, three – goals manifesting, things growing, etc. Here, especially in cartomancy divination, correspondences can vary on the context of what the number is paired with. For example, two of hearts may symbolise new love but two of clubs may indicate a power struggle. Numerology is also popularly associated with the concept of 'angel numbers', a term coined by Doreen Virtue,[5] which posits that angels communicate with us through repeated number symbology (111, 222, etc.). Whether or not you ascribe to this belief, keep in mind the dangers of confirmation bias, of which is discussed at length later in Chapter 7 of this book.

Knot magic entails exactly what it says, it is magic involving the use of knots. A widely known knot magic spell is the "Witches Ladder", whereby you chant as you tie nine knots into a piece of string or rope. This type of magic is just that, focusing on a magical goal and imbuing that into your spell by tying a knot.

There are many different types of practical magic, as there are countless methods of folk magic. Many of these labels for practical magic are simply adopted based upon the function of the spell, for example, poppet magic, sachet magic, candle magic, etc. Some magical practices don't necessarily have an overarching label given to them, such as how movements can infer intention; deosil or clockwise is used to attract or brings things in, whereas widdershins or anti-clockwise is used to repel or banish. All in all, labels such as these described above are not prescriptive and not to get bogged down on necessarily but are also helpful when specifying the type of magic that we are performing.

Types of Magical Workings

The term **spell** has a rather basic definition, of which the following is preferred here: a magical formula of both conscious intention and action, aimed to produce a desired effect in the world or influence a change. It is purposefully broad, as individual practitioners will understandably have varying approaches to spells, but also, a variety of practice can fall within the concept of spells.

Whilst a spell can indeed be a ritual, not all rituals are spells. A **ritual** is further a magical formula of both conscious intention and action, aimed to produce a desired effect in the world or influence a change, but can relate more to ceremonial spiritual ambitions.

An **incantation** is a set of spoken words, mostly said out loud in order to produce a magical effect. The tone with which you speak out loud these words (in whatever language) can correspond to its effect.

Charms are also something which have a relatively broad definition. A charm is simply something which has been imbued with magic. More heavily present in folk magical practices, charms can include any object and a lot of spells involve the creation of charms.

Amulets are also something traditionally used for protection. They are often used interchangeably with **talisman**, which is a charm imbued with magic to manifest or attract. The key difference is in the magical intention.

A **sigil** is a (usually) handmade symbol drafted from a particular magical intention. This symbol is meant to be powered through an action such as burning it, but can also be utilised like a talisman.

Jinxes are typically baneful spells that cause a mild annoyance or bad luck to a target. They are designed to cause harm (as per the defining feature of baneful magic), however, they are often not very severely harmful. They are spells often done to trigger an inconvenience on the person and are less durable as a spell.

Hexes are spells designed to inflict small amounts of harm. They are often employed to make a person's life worse in small to medium severity, as opposed to completely destroying their life. A hex is usually meant to last a shorter amount of time than a larger baneful spell such as a curse, and often the right magical protections enforced will block them anyway.

Curses are spells used to inflict severe harm. As opposed to jinxes or hexes where the baneful magic is intentionally lighter and more short-term, the effects of a curse are usually intended to be more long-lasting and disruptive to the person's life. Curses are often not done lightly and typically performed when the person really deserves it. Though protection magic such as wards can block curses, the stronger the curse the harder it will be to deflect. It is not unusual for protections to not be able to withstand curses.

Chapter 4

Foundational Magical Practices

It is tempting to dive deep into performing spells but taking the time to home in on your foundational magical skills can be very enriching for your path. It builds a craft or path that has longevity and is sustainable, as having the basics down sets you up for a variety of more advanced practices. In any case, magical paths such as witchcraft, are so much more than just performing spells or rituals. The simple basic practices can often be the most enlightening for some. What's most important to remember is that we all have the ability to perform magic and utilise our inner power, but certain practices can strength this muscle and improve our spiritual fitness.

Meditation

Meditation is a practice that is thousands of years old, having ancient ties across various traditions, but notably from the Upanishads (Vedanta) of Hindu philosophy, Taoist China, Buddhist India and ancient Egypt. Defining meditation can be a little difficult as there are so many different ways one can do so, however, as a whole, meditation (dhyana) is an ancient practice, utilising focused attention or awareness on a particular object, topic or feeling to promote relaxation, stillness and calm and to enhance spiritual or personal growth. Many people may instantly think of meditating as needing to be sat in a cross-legged lotus asana position, chanting a particular mantra such as "om". Whilst these aspects of meditating do have cultural significance from certain traditions, it is not the only way one can meditate. You can be in any position that feels comfortable to you to meditate, some people prefer meditating lying down or standing up, others prefer meditative walks or meditative movements such as dancing. So long as you have that state of calm, awareness and focused attention, you are meditating. It seems as though meditation is a barrier for lots of magical practitioners. You find people being adamant that they cannot meditate or get their mind to be still, but the truth is, the very act of trying is performing meditation. You are focusing your attention on something, and that is enough, and of course, practice makes perfect. If you fit meditation or any type of meditative activities in your regular routine, you will become better at it and will be able to feel the positive effects of meditation.

What also can help is understanding that there are innumerable ways to meditate, so if one way does not work for you, perhaps try experiment with another. Meditation is simply a broad term for an array of techniques or practices that involve focus and attention on an object, feeling or sensation. Just taking five minutes out of your day to sit and quieten your mind (even if it's not going how you'd like) is meditating. One of the simplest meditations a magical practitioner can start with is a simple equal rotation meditation. It is based on a pranayama technique called Sama Vritti (square wave pattern) and all it involves is inhaling on 4 counts (puraka), holding this breath for 4 counts (antar kumbhaka), exhaling on 4 counts (rechaka) and holding this breath exhalation for 4 counts (bahya kumbhaka).[1]

Incorporating meditation into your regular magical routine can have significant impacts on your practice. Not only is regularly meditating known to have positive effects on our physical and mental health, but it can drastically aid your spiritual practice, particularly in improving one's ability to cast effective magic, home in on one's intuition and communicate with spirits. As we better our ability to focus and still our mind, we are more capable of focusing on a magical goal, setting that intention and homing in on that magic.

Visualisation

Visualisation is something often employed in conjunction with meditation but is also a spiritual technique used to (what more new age focused spiritual traditions call) "manifest" and charge spell objects.

Visualisation is the simple act of being able to conjure imagery in your mind's eye or "witch's eye" which it is often otherwise referred to as. For example, its thinking of an apple, perhaps closing your eyes, and being able to see that apple in your mind, not necessarily as a real visual stimulus in the physical world, but in your mental world. It is a very powerful tool to have under your magical toolbelt as it allows us, as magical practitioners, to picture clearly what we desire and focus in on that goal. Keeping strong visualisations in mind during the spellwork process is an act of charging the spell in itself (as discussed in Chapter 5), but also adds to its power. You can further think of it in a psychological sense, it gets us thinking about what we want and makes us motivated to work towards that goal. The more you have in your mind what you want to achieve and be able to see it in action in your mind, the more likely you will align your behaviour with that goal. I am a strong believer that just because we can explain how things work (in this case, basic psychology), does not mean that it's not magic.

The difficulty is that not everyone can visualise in the traditional sense of the word. It isn't very accessible for those who have aphantasia; the inability to create mental imagery or those with mental health difficulties that make things like visualising harder than usual (such as ADHD). If this struggle or any others apply to you, there is no need to worry as there are boundless alternatives to visualisation. Rather than focusing on creating pictures, try to focus on feelings and emotions. If you are casting a prosperity spell for a raise on your income, conjure up that feeling of contentment stemming from financial security or perhaps joy and excitement after achieving something great. There doesn't have to be any images involved, just simply maintaining a meditative focus on those appropriate feelings. If thinking of any past memories helps in this process, by all means utilise them.

Grounding and Centring

Grounding and centring are two practical energy work techniques that can really help you strengthen your magical and meditative abilities for your craft. They are often mistaken as the same practice, but they do have different goals in mind and accomplish slightly different things.

Grounding as a concept was developed largely in the somatic psychotherapy field through the work of psychologist Alexander Lowen and his theory of bioenergetics.[2] Grounding follows the idea of connecting your body to the earth, the energy flowing from your body to the ground, helping us to stay "grounded" and releasing what no longer serves us. In psychotherapeutic theory, grounding offers a sense of safety and allows us to be more in touch with all parts of our body[3] and can be very helpful for those dealing with depression or anxiety. Grounding keeps us in the moment, when it's easy to lose track of life. There are times when we get in our heads too much, from overthinking or over-worrying, grounding helps us connect to that earth energy and brings us back down into our surroundings.

So, you can see how in magical practice, it can be vital. Not only helping us connect to the energy of the earth and relieve ourselves of any excess energy in the body, but also using the earth as a source of energy, allowing us to power our spells and charms. Before casting a spell or performing a ritual, making sure that we are grounded can assist in improving our focus for the magic. Grounding can be especially important after we perform a spell, as it allows us to recharge when the performing of magic can, at times, be a little draining.

Over the years, methods by which we can ground have been shared and like with most spiritual practices, what works best for you individually will vary from person to person. Though, simple ways anyone can ground can include brewing a hot drink and sipping it with some meditative focus or sitting outside and paying close attention to your natural surroundings. This includes not using any device that can distract or focus or mindfulness. Exercising or more physically interactive hobbies, such as gardening or sewing, can be great grounding practices too, as they help you keep connected to the physical realm and that earth energy. A method commonly shared in spiritual spaces incorporates tree visualisations, where one sits in a meditative lotus asana and imagines the base of their spine as roots digging deep into the earth. With each breath, one takes time to feel the energy travelling up the spine and extending upwards, sweeping back down into the earth. This is a very potent technique; however, it heavily relies on the skill of visualisation, which many are not able to do. The follow exercise is offered as an alternative, suitable for many.

Exercise 2 – Waterfall Grounding

This exercise shared is taken from bioenergetic psychotherapy[4] and only takes a few minutes to perform.

- Start by standing upright with your feet placed hip-width apart (I find this works best barefoot).
- Make sure your toes are pointed slightly inwards to help stretch some of those muscles.
- Slowly bend forward and touch your fingertips on the ground in front of you. It's okay (and encouraged if you need to) bend your knees during this process. Be sure to not put any weight on your hands though, it should still be placed more on your feet, the fingers are for anchoring yourself.

- Let go of all tension in your neck and head and let them hang loose.
- Breathe deeply, in through your nose and out through your mouth. Stay present with your breathing throughout.
- Let yourself hang down for however long you need or want to, but 1–5 minutes is a good amount of time. Be sure to come back up slowly.

Whilst centring is a different practice, it is also a psychological technique involving the use of energy to find your "inner centre" and help promote a sense of calm and focus. It is believed to have derived from Aikido, a Japanese ancient martial arts practice which uses meditation and breath work to harmonise the spirit and centre our emotions.[5] In psychotherapy, centring can help one find peace within ourselves, for those struggling with anxiety, intrusive thoughts or generally just overwhelmed. Centring helps us bring calm to our emotions, and process how and why we are experiencing them. Centring in a spiritual sense, refers to our mental and physical state of mind and connects ourselves to the moment by helping align our inner energies. It involves stabilising these energies and collecting them into a central focal point. This as a practice can become largely helpful for a magical practice as you can then direct this collected energy out into the world, a magical object, etc., in a spell or ritual.

Centring is a little simpler in practice and can be done through basic breathing techniques such as the Sama Vritti pranayama as mentioned prior. Any mindfulness meditation will promote a sense of calm and focus, and thus centre you very efficiently. Another favourite of many visualisers is incorporating imagery of prismatic light entering the top of your head, from the divine in the sky. This light connects to your centre, infusing you with stillness and balance.

Exercise 3 – Simple Sensory Centring

This centring technique doesn't involve any fancy energy work or visualisations, it only requires yourself and the use of your senses.

- Sit down comfortably somewhere, outdoors is best or perhaps just facing an open window.
- Close your eyes and focus on your breathing until you feel a sense of calm.
- Open your eyes and closely observe what's around you.
- In your head or saying out loud, identify 5 things that you can see.
- Then, identify 4 things you can hear.
- Identify 3 things you can feel.
- Identify 2 things you can smell.
- Identify 1 thing you can taste.
- Sit in this moment, reflecting on these sensations and experiencing them all.

Cleansing, Purification and Banishing

Cleansing, purification and banishing are three base magical practices that are foundational for any magical practitioner's path. They're sometimes confused together and used interchangeably but they are three distinct practices.

Cleansing is the art of removing any unwanted stagnant or lingering energy from a particular object, place or person. It is easy to think of it like cleaning in the mundane sense – cleansing is the equivalent to lightly dusting, tidying the room and putting clothes away. We are getting the place ready for what we want to use it for, resetting, so-to-speak. In magical practice, cleansing is employed for numerous things. Cleansing our magical tools before we use them or cleansing our bodies or spaces if it feels "off", to list a couple examples. We cleanse so that any of the existing spiritual miasma or energy does not affect us in what we want to practice. If one performs a spell using a jar that has been already used in a prior spell, it is worth cleansing the jar to rid of any energy or magic that can interfere with the new spell.

Purification is a similar process, and it is the art of removing any energy from a particular object, place or person. Using the cleaning analogy, it's not just lightly dusting, it's getting out that hoover and vacuuming the floors, moving the furniture around and getting every piece of dirt in every nook and cranny. We purify our spaces, objects and bodies when we need to reset completely and when there is a particularly strong energy affecting us.

What really differentiates the two is the intention. Have a clear understanding of what you are trying to do and adapt the method and goal by which you cleanse or purify to which one you choose. When choosing your method, your options are endless and many different cultural folk traditions have their preferred methods. Do whatever works best for you and what you enjoy doing, as there are no set ways to cleanse or purify. However, some brief examples are included here for guidance:

- Use of smoke – burning incense, which can come in loose form (a mixture of resin, loose herbs and other natural materials), or as premade cones or sticks. Specific plant allies associated with cleansing or purification can be petitioned to assist you in magic.
- Use of sound – playing music, drumming, ringing bells, singing; these are all less obvious examples of air magic, and help shake up the energy or spirit of the place.
- Use of movement – dancing, using a broom or besom to sweep out the energy or interfering spirits.

- Use of certain ingredients as they are – for example, a bowl of salt not only absorbs the moisture from the air, but is also said to absorb the stagnant, disruptive energy. If you enjoy the use of crystals, Selenite is said to be inherently cleansing.
- Use of liquid – many folk traditions employ the use of sacred waters to sprinkle around a place, object or person, to cleanse or purify them/it. You could create your own blends of appropriately diluted essential oils associated with cleansing or purification into water.
- Use of visualisation – visualisations of cleansing light is often utilised by practitioners in conjunction with other physical methods, though visualisation alone can work just as well. It works alongside the energy model, using visualisation as a spiritual tool to manipulate the energy in a room or around an object/person you are intended to cleanse or purify.

Banishing, on the other hand, is slightly more nuanced. Usually, it refers to the process of actively getting rid of a particular spirit or maybe perhaps, a rather large accumulation of unwanted energy in a particular area. There is an argument of semantics, on cleansing and purification can be described as banishing energy, but more often than not, banishing refers to spirit work. Plenty of magic in ceremonial occult traditions is dedicated to banishing rituals, with a more notable example being the "Lesser Banishing Ritual of the Pentagram," a famous magical rite from the Golden Dawn. This is a formula that involves different aspects, including the evocation of four archangels at certain cardinal points.[6]

Divination

A further foundational magical practice is the utilisation of divination. Divination is the art of navigating the future, deciphering the unknown and introspecting through spiritual means. It is an ancient concept, used not just by magical practitioners, but those who would rather consider themselves spiritual or those who would understand it as simple traditional custom. We divine to understand outcomes of spells, to communicate with spirits, to reflect on our wellbeing and our future, and for many other reasons. Having at least one (two is best) method of divination can be vital for the practice of magic.

Needless to say, there are thousands, if not hundreds of thousands, of methods of divination. From looking at the clouds in the sky (nephomancy), to the use of fortune-telling cards (cartomancy), even the action of shuffling songs on a playlist (shufflemancy).[7] In modern day, the most accessible forms of divination include tarot, oracle, pendulum dowsing and scrying. Cartomancy in general, be it through the use of tarot, oracle cards or simple playing cards, can be a slight learning curve. Tarot in particular has lots of layered correspondences to the cards and is dependent too on the system used (the Rider-Waite Smith deck system is the one most employed in commercial tarot decks). Scrying, however, is a simple and archaic practice that anyone can perform. Simply by closing your eyes, letting your eyes glaze over into the darkness of your eyelids, maintain a calm and still mind, and let any images or shapes form.

Usually divination involves asking a question, performing the method, and analysing the answer based on the options given to you. More often than not, it's important to ask the right question, which can be further dependent on the type of divination you are using. Pendulum dowsing is the simple act of holding a string/cord/chain with a heavy object on the other end with your fingers and letting it sway without any conscious movement of your hand. This can vary for the individual, but usually clockwise is yes and anti-clockwise is no. Here with pendulum dowsing, the question you ask is reliant on a yes or no answer, so ask your question carefully. Cartomancy methods can involve lots of cards each with assigned meanings and layered symbology, capable of producing more open-ended and complicated answers. Therefore, being specific with your question is preferred.

Finding and developing a divinatory practice is so useful for your magical path, as it will help you advance your spellwork and navigate those murky spiritual waters. Take your time to try out different techniques and find one that suits you best.

Protection and Safety

Though at times overstated, it will always reign true that being safe and making sure you are prepared for what you are going to do is essential. Magic isn't always sunshine and rainbows and if you're a spirit worker, you'll know that not all spirits are friendly and welcoming.

You can look at protection or safety from two sides – mundane and magical. The mundane aspects are just as important as the magical, and often overlooked at times where it seems rather obvious or boring. However, precautionary measures such as fire safety will always be vital to follow through. Be very careful with lighting candles with untrimmed wicks that can produce large flames, or candle holders made out of flammable material or naked flames adjacent to flammable material. Always be sure that your magical set up avoids any imminent danger, as fire can be ferocious and can spread very quickly if one is even the slightest bit distracted.

On the topic of using fire in spells, there are a lot of people who state that you shouldn't blow out your candle and let it burn all the way down every time. This is not a hard-and-fast rule as many make it out to be and can be entirely dependent on personal preference or the type of spell you are performing. Some spells will necessitate burning the candle for a longer period of time, especially if the magical goal is quite a large one that spans over a series of days. Seven-day candles are recommended for these sorts of spells, which are left to burn alone for long periods of time. Though, these candles are not immune to danger; ones sold in witchcraft shops are often overpacked with herbs and other flammable material. When these catch on fire, they produce large flames, producing large amounts of heat and thus, can cause the glass to crack and the candle to explode. Always be careful when dressing candles with whatever material and leaving them alone for long periods of time. Where there is a need to leave your candle to burn, always keep it in eyeshot and in a safe location. There may be times you need to extinguish the flame but do not want to finish the spell, instead you can decide to blow or snuff out the flame with the conscious intention of pausing the magic. Simply relight it later, restating your magical intention and even recharging the candle if you so desire.

There is, of course, the safety aspect of using plants and herbs in your spells. Especially considering how witchcraft and other magical traditions have long, rich and interesting histories intertwined with the use of poisonous and toxic plants, such as Monkshood (*Aconitum napellus*), Deadly Nightshade (*Atropa belladonna*) and Henbane (*Hyoscyamus niger*). Lots of traditions, especially in Traditional Witchcraft, incorporate the use of these plants into spells and ritual practices. It may sound obvious, but always be careful with handling these sorts of plants in your practice, unless you are 100% sure about what you are doing and in your research.

Many magical practitioners are plant lovers and are, what is often referred to as, "green witches." This can involve foraging and wildcrafting your own plants for spells, which is a fantastic way to bond with the spirit/energy of the plant to power your spells, however, many forget that foraging (including botanical species identification) is a skill that takes time to perfect. I believe that many tend to commit a naturalistic fallacy when looking at nature, believing that just because its natural, it must be 'good' or harmless. The reality is nature is just nature; it is beautiful and amazing, but also brutal, powerful and terrifying. Don't underestimate it, especially when foraging for your own plants for your magical practice.

It is always going to be worth triple checking through various methods what the species of the plant you are using is. Nowadays there are many highly useful mobile apps that help the lay person identify a plant, but they are not fool proof. Many plant species have lookalikes, where there are numerous plants that resemble each other but are different in the effect they can have on you. One example native to the UK is Hemlock (*Conium maculatum*), a poisonous white flowered umbellifer plant that (to the untrained eye) can look very similar to other members of the same family, the *Apiaceae* family, that are relatively harmless such as Cow Parsley (*Anthriscus sylvestris*). Unless you are highly skilled in botany, always use more than one method when identifying species. This might include using an app to start off with, double checking in a field guide or plant key and then checking in some online forums where people who are trained in species identification can verify it for you.

In addition, as many of us know, it is not just physical protection that is necessary in a magical path, but spiritual protection too. Whether you believe in spirits or energy, like with nature, neither are inherently good or harmless. You can come across spirits that are like leeches and will drain you completely and you can get energy sent your way that is malefic and intentionally harmful. You needn't get panicked if you are a beginner stepping into magic for the first time, as it is highly unlikely people will be flinging curses at you at the start. Honestly, curses in general do tend to be rare, but people do indeed perform them. My advice is that it's not worth getting stressed or paranoid about it, however, knowing and implementing a few protection measures, just in case, can't hurt.

Your options for magical protection will depend on the model of magic you generally ascribe to. If you adopt the energy model, shielding may be your go-to, whereby you form energetic shields to protect yourself from external disruption. This can be through manipulating energy and forming visualisations such as an orb surrounding what/who you are trying to protect. My favourite method when trying to protect myself against disruptive and harmful energy is visualisation of Bramble (*Rubus fruticosus*) scrub growing around my body, defending whatever harm comes my way with its prickly thorns. If you are more of an animist, an option for protection can include appealing to plant spirits as a protective ward. This is especially helpful for home protection, and enlisting the help of potted plants placed at the corners of your home to protect you from any harm sent your way. Apotropaic magic has existed for centuries and there are plenty of resources out there to guide you further, which can be found recommended at the back of this book.

Chapter 5

Crafting Spells

Putting some herbs in a bag or lighting a candle sounds simple enough, but there is much more to crafting a spell than the physical action alone. There is so much to consider when crafting a spell, all the layers that build up and power the magic; ingredient correspondences, magical timings, charging the spell and more. All these things can have real impacts on the efficacy of your spell. I find that spells generally work best when incorporating five key components to the crafting process: the goal, the ingredients, the methodology, charging the spell, the action and praxis, and the disposal (using the acronym GIMCA may help you to remember). When taking into consideration these five aspects, our spells can be tailored more specifically to our needs and desires. Adding the detail and allowing for our spells to be more precise to a situation, makes them more likely to be effective as it is something we are putting a lot of care and thought into.

The Goal

This is arguably the most important aspect of the spell, identifying first what it is that you want to achieve. Since magic is influencing a change, specifying what change we want influenced is key. Looking to the magical intentions outlined in Chapter 1, reflect deeply on what it is you are turning to magic for. If you are looking to increase your financial income, it is likely prosperity magic will be what you are after. If you are looking to guard against people who are saying mean things about you, you'll be choosing protection magic as your goal. This is the beginning step; take a look at the situation you are in and identify what type of magic you think you may need.

Once this understanding is in place, think about why you need this change to happen. Why are you looking to increase your financial income – is there a big expense that needs to be paid soon? Are you saving up for a house? Do you just want to live more comfortably? Dive into some introspection and analyse what the reason is behind stepping to magic for this desire in the first place. Reflecting on the background context will only strengthen and build your magic.

Through this process, it also helps you take into consideration all the non-magical options before jumping head-first into magic as a cure-all solution. Magic is extremely helpful and a powerful tool, but in a lot of scenarios, simply working through and putting in some special effort can resolve a problem quicker than you realise. You could do a banishing spell to get rid of those nasty gossipers, but you could also try communicating with them first and opening up some mature conversation. Healing magic can be extremely potent, but if you think something is wrong, it might be wise to put consulting a medical professional on the top of the list, before the spell. Sometimes running through these mundane options first can be massively useful, for everyone's sake in the scenario.

When the understanding of *what, why* and *how* of your goal is agreed upon, it is time to put together a sentence that will be the main magical intention behind the spell. The spell intention is one that should be fairly specific. Magical goals that state desires such as "I am protected" isn't always enough to achieve those desires in actuality. Protected from what? From whom? Your spell goal doesn't have to be a novel, however, addressing the context in the magical intention can really help the magic work more effectively. Using this example, you may expand it to "I am protected from the evil eye", or "I am protected from disruptive energy whilst I work". Specificity is key.

Also, many practitioners are adamant that writing your goal in present tense works more efficiently than phrasing it in future tense. It does hold some truth, as going forward with your magic as you are making it happen currently, assists in its success. "I get a pay rise" tends to sound better than "I will get a pay rise", as the former sounds more assertive and current, as if it's happening right now as you are willing it so. Arguably this is just needless superstition but phrasing your goal in the future tense is almost like you will be always willing it to happen. But the real trick is to go with your gut, as this will only certify your goal and strengthen it.

Remember that you don't have to go exactly by the spell book all the time. It can be helpful when you are starting out casting spells for the first time, but keep in mind that you can adapt your spellcrafting to what feels most intuitive to you. If your magical practice or craft hasn't got any essence of your own magic in it, then your spells are bound to fail.

The Ingredients

This part is where it can get more complicated. What does one include in their spell? Realistically, the magical practitioner can include anything in their spellcraft. There is no measure which determines which objects are magical enough to be included in a working. Spellcraft is an art, as is the practice of magic itself, so there is literally no manner for practicing it so there is no wrong way to perform a spell is a little misleading, but fundamentally it is true. Everyone has their own moral code on what type of spells they'd personally feel comfortable performing, and we all have varying levels of accessibility to certain materials. Understanding that energy or spirit lies in everything, and magic can be found anywhere, leads you with plenty of options on what to include in your spellcraft. That being said, of course, there are some staples that take up most witches' or magical practitioners' cupboards. These can include plants, rocks, bones, candles, oils, incenses, etc. All of these ingredients are known to have inherent magical qualities (law of correspondence), which is why they are commonly used in spells.

The ingredients you include do not have to be complicated. Within much of the witchcraft and occult literature out there, you will find recipes for spells that require all sorts of fancy herbs, crystals, oils, and such. More often than not, the average person finds these very inaccessible. Especially for those who are on a budget, do not live in a place which has a lot of shopping options, or simply avoids the consumerist lifestyle. Regardless, it is worth nothing that there is no single spell recipe for the magical practitioner, and you do not have to include those non-native plants that require being shipped halfway across the world to you – you can use what is already around you. You do not need to spend ridiculous amounts of money on minerals mined in countries that face human rights issues and exploit their workers.[1] If anything, it is highly encouraged to lead a more sustainable and environmentally conscious magical practice.

So, if you are feeling stuck on what to include in your spellcraft, look no further than what is physically around you. Here is a list of ideas for spell ingredients that can likely be found around the average person's house:

- Trinkets such as animal figurines or small boxes can be altar décor or spell tools.
- Herbs and spices from the kitchen are just as magically potent as foraged plants or plants specifically bought for magical usage.
- Houseplants can act as plant spirit allies and can be use in plant magic too, e.g., plant wards.
- Tealight candles can be especially useful and potent in candle magic.
- A pack of playing cards are perfect for cartomancy and can also be used in magic.

- String, thread or rope can be utilised for knot magic and many such customs are found in various folk magic traditions.
- The preparation and cooking of food can be a magical act in itself! Kitchen witchcraft is immensely popular and there have been many books that detail its practice.

Furthermore, as outlined in Chapter 2, what someone includes in their spells will depend on how they view the world, magic, and their spell ingredients. Animists may view spell ingredients a having a spirit, so when including them in a spell, it is an act of bonding with the spirit. Energy model enthusiasts will connect more to the energy of the ingredients instead. Some (including yours truly) connect to both! So, when picking what to include, your options are endless, as long as you can adequately connect to that object's spirit and asks for its help. This is why it is beneficial to reflect on your magical worldview as you look to advance your craft or spellwork.

Exercise 4 – Discovering Magical Correspondences

In this process of using whatever is at your disposal in your spellcraft, you may come across items that you feel called to use, but do not know their magical correspondence. There is a reason why many modern magical practitioners just use ingredients listed in spell books, as they usually come with well-established correspondences, that often have a long-standing SPG or VPG.

However, as stated before, the practice of magic is a personal journey and more often than not, a completely subjective experience. Whether you follow the energy, spirit, or psychology model or something else entirely, you can intuitively divine your own personal magical correspondences and do not always have to rely on books to tell you what they are. Utilising sensory information and research can tell you a lot about an object's spiritual nature and factors you may consider when discovering magical correspondences can include colour, shape, pattern, smell, taste, but also history, folklore and medicine. What you use will depend on what you are trying to discover the magical correspondence for, but let's use an example.

Say you found a common wayside plant that you want to include in your spell, but there is little information in store-bought plant magic books that detail its magical usage. Start off by getting yourself in a meditative state; take some deep, slow breaths and focus on the plant. Concentrate on its features, what colours make up the plant? If it is mostly green, is it more of a warm green or cooler green? What feelings does it invoke thinking about this? If there are any blossoms, what colour are they? Jot down any feelings, emotions, thoughts, or imagery that springs to mind when you are reflecting on the colours.

You can do the same for the shape of the plant, are the leaves round? Elongated? Do they have sharp edges? Hairy stems? Do any of these features conjure forth any symbolism to you? Worry not if it's a bit quirky, nobody is here judging the associations that come forth to you, as it is all completely valid and authentic to you.

If you know the species of the plant, but are still to find magical information about it, try researching into folklore and historical uses of the plant, which may include medicinal herbalism. Much of what the plant used to be used for is carried forward in magical correspondences, for example, St. John's Wort (*Hypericum perforatum*) traditionally used for treating low mood (always consult a medical professional before self-medicating) and magically symbolising joy and happiness.

This exercise won't necessarily see results in just one sitting and remember that it is completely okay if these things take time. Your spirituality isn't a race!

Outside of the inner components of the spell, there is the outer, container part of the spell to think about. This may be a charm bag or sachet, glass jar (often called a "witch bottle"), poppet, or even more mundane features such as a candle holder or bowl. It's important to think about these too, as these are the structures of the spell itself that hold all the pieces together. My advice is to use what you have on hand. It is tempting to batch order a bunch of tiny spell jars that seem to be very popular amongst online displays of witchcraft, but really this is unnecessary. Rather than doing this, you can save your old sauce jars from your kitchen, clean them well, purify them and use them in your spells. You can even use spare pieces of fabric or material such as old socks and make them into poppets or charm bags for your spells. You just need a needle and thread and/or string and a little time put aside for some crafting.

Most of the time, one will find themselves choosing a structural component that aligns with their spell intention. To give some examples, practitioners may go to candle magic for the spells which they need to happen as soon as possible, to align with the element of fire's quick and fierce energy or will utilise a bowl for prosperity magic that is more of a long-term goal, as bowls can be associated with the water element and its correspondences to continuous movement and flow.

The Methodology

By now, you should know what you want to be achieved and have a rough idea of what ingredients you have at your disposal for the spell. Now is the time to start planning when and how you're going to perform it, and there's numerous factors to bear in mind. Realistically, you can perform your spell at any point. When the situation necessitates it, you need to do the magic and can't always wait until the perfectly astrologically timed moment. However, timing your magic with astrology and other external metaphysical factors can definitely give your magic a boost, especially if your spell has a specific intention or it's a rather large spell.

Timing your spells with the phases of the Moon (lunar magic) has had a strong place in magical traditions for years. If you're performing a prosperity spell to bring more money into your life, conducting the spell when the current Moon phase is in its Waxing stage aligns well, as the Waxing phase symbolises growth and attraction. Likewise, if you're looking to banish something from your life, performing the magic on a Waning moon phase is more ideal as this phase symbolises things decreasing, or removal and repelling. Big spells are often reserved for a Full Moon, where the magic is most potent and for the New Moon, cleansings or setting goals for the following Moon cycle is reserved.

Instead of using the phases of the Moon, many magical practitioners incorporate planetary magic for their spell timings. Planetary magic is something seen in almost all forms and traditions of magic and is very versatile. In terms of planetary timing your spells, it can involve using a planetary energy in accordance with a day of the week or the planetary hour of the day. For example, if you want to perform a self-love spell, you may want to conduct it on a Friday, for Venus; Venus as a planet is associated with many things, but most popularly, love. The following is a non-exhaustive list of the seven classical planets and their magical associations that you can implement in your magical timings:

- **Moon** (element: Water, day: Monday) – trance work, divination, dreams, the unconscious, glamours.
- **Mars** (element: Fire, day: Tuesday) – courage, anger, passion, strength, ego, uncrossings, reversals.
- **Mercury** (element: Air, day: Wednesday) – business, communication, memory, travel, focus.
- **Jupiter** (element: Air/Water, day: Thursday) – health, fortune, finance, luck, politics, expansion, prosperity spells.

- **Venus** (element: Earth, day: Friday) – beauty, love, self-confidence, sexuality, fertility, art, friendships, self-development.
- **Saturn** (element: Earth, day: Saturday) – wisdom, discipline, time, formation, duty, bindings, banishment spells, protection spells.
- **Sun** (element: Fire, day: Sunday) – joy, wealth, success, personal power, setting intentions, beginning projects.

Other magical timings can include looking to astrology and what zodiacal sign is ruling what planet, or popular neopagan solar festivals such as the equinoxes and solstices. Recommendations for further resources on these topics can be found in the back of the book.

Outside of timing, another important aspect of the methodology section of the spell is thinking about where it's going to live and do its magic. Where you spell stays can be a big part of how efficiently the magic works, for example, keeping a travel protection charm on your person as you travel. Especially if it's a more long-term spell whereby the magic is to be working over a longer period of time, then you'll want it placed in an ideal location which corresponds to the goal at hand. To give some ideas, if it's a spell relating to prosperity, keep the spell near where your sources of income are, such as a work desk or if it's a spell for another person, they may want it in their vicinity. Of course, this doesn't always apply, for example, candle spells you'll likely want to perform and keep at your altar as this is more practical and safer. Going even further, with spells like this, they're usually done pretty quickly and don't require them to be out for long periods of time. This is where we can plan how we're going to dispose of it (of which is detailed further in Chapter 7), but in short, you can dispose of your spell in a way which is most environmentally friendly but also accessible to you.

The Charging of the Spell

Charging goes beyond the simple act of compiling objects together and infuses the creation with magical power. When we perform spells, we are creating a magical object or ritual that aims to power our goal into reality, but this power needs to come from somewhere. We charge our spells, usually by entering trance-like states of consciousness and tapping into the magic to power the spell. As established before, depending on your model of magic you ascribe to, your magic will come from a specific source.

If you're following the spirit model, here is where you'll plan to petition a spirit to aid in your magical working. This can involve numerous spiritual actions that are often tradition dependent, but more simply, it can be a simple invocation or prayer to a particular spirit. You'll likely want to give an offering in exchange for your working to be done, which again, can be tradition or spirit dependent. Some spirits like certain foods, drinks, objects or even devotional acts, so bare that in mind if you do call upon a spirit to power your magic and fulfil your desire. Whilst I am of the opinion that spirit work is not a practice exclusive to more advanced practitioners (as many state), it is also important to acknowledge that the spirit world is not always a friendly place or easy path to navigate. Make sure you have your basic protections up and are familiar with the spirit you are appealing to if you are asking for help. You wouldn't expect a random stranger on the street to do you a big, personal favour out of nowhere, so why expect a spirit to do the same? Building a relationship with your spirits is key for getting them to help you in your magic, and this can be a simple process. Researching into their cultural origins, setting up a small shrine or altar to them, saying regular prayers or using means such as divination or spirit flight to communicate with them are all actions which help you connect to a spirit. See the Recommended Reading section as enclosed for further resources on this.

If we're adopting the energy model, then the process by which we charge our spells is through manipulating energy. Here, energy exists in all things and as energy cannot be created or destroyed, it's not necessarily plucking energy out of thin air, but manipulating what is already there. This may be utilising the energies of certain natural materials, for example, tapping into the protective energy of Rowan (*Sorbus aucuparia*) to charge a protection spell, or utilising a planetary energy as outlined in our methodology. There are boundless external sources that magical practitioners draw from, from more intricate astrological sources to something as simple as using the energy of a candle flame to boost a magical intention.

Another common energetic charging method is simply drawing upon your own energy as a means to power the spell. Utilising kinetic means to build up your own energy can power a spell, and it is a highly accessible method of charging. Spiritual cultures and traditions across the world have incorporated movement, dance, singing and the like, to accumulate energy within oneself for rituals or ceremonies, and the same can be done with spells. A personal favourite practice is to employ sound (be it music, drumming or nature soundscapes) to increase my energy for a spell. It is especially powerful if the sound corresponds with the nature of the intention, for example, playing uplifting melodies for positivity or abundance spells.

Exercise 5 – Creating a Raising Energy Playlist

Music is such a powerful tool. One song can invoke such strong emotions, feelings, thoughts, memories and so much more. To me, this is pure magic. It speaks to how much music can move us and it can also help us move our magic too. If you're a music lover like myself, then this exercise may be quite straightforward for you, but no matter if not.

Using a music app such as Spotify, Soundcloud or YouTube, or rather if these don't appeal to you, grab some blank CDs and a CD burner, and create your very own magical mixtape. Compile a list of songs that build up your energy. This could be some really happy, upbeat pop tunes that you love to sing to, or some hard rock that you love jamming to. Whatever you prefer is ultimately best, as this will be what moves you most. You may also be inclined to make a playlist based upon the aesthetic of magic; for example, popular trends of witchcraft aesthetics usually incorporate music from bands such as Fleetwood Mac or Sixpence None the Richer. If this gets you in the mood to practice magic and allows that energy to build up inside you, then there's no shame in indulging into the aesthetics side of the craft. You could also tailor a playlist to specific goal intentions, maybe if you're doing some banishing work, you might want to curate a playlist of angsty heartbreak songs or self-empowerment ballads. Don't be afraid to allow your inner child to run wild with this one, because this exercise is designed for you to have fun! Think of it like making a gym playlist, you want to add music which aligns with the exercises you'll be doing.

When you have crafted your magical playlist, all that is required is to play it when you are crafting your spell. Let yourself get really into the music, feel every word spoken and focus in on every note that flows. Let your body move the way it feels called to and home in on that energy that starts to build up. Once this energy has risen and you can feel it surging through you, now is the time to direct that into your spell you are crafting. This can be as simple as through a push of the hands, visualising that energy shooting out of your vessel into the magical object, or you could make use of a magical tool, such as a wand or stang.

Sealing the spell is a practice employed at this stage too, where it essentially finalises the spell, separating the magical moment from the mundane. It can also be seen as a way of charging depending on how you look at it. Sealing a spell can be as simple as stating "so mote it be" or "and it is done". My personal favourite is "I wind, I bind, the spell be mine". You can seal a spell literally, by tying a knot, around your spell jar or charm bag, for example, or kissing your spell creation. My advice is simply to end your spell here whichever way feels most intuitive to you, there aren't really any 'wrong' ways to seal a spell.

The Action

At this point, you've likely put together a spell, charged and sealed it and the magic has henceforth been sent out into the universe. We don't stop here – now, we do the work.

We know that there is more to spells than just wishing for the best, we have to make sure our actions align with our magical goals. In our goal making step, we established that we need to understand where and how the magic is going to work. If you're performing a prosperity spell to attract some money, where is the money most likely to come from? If it's from a raise in your salary, think about whether your employer is likely to give you a pay rise at this moment in time. Reflect on your behaviour at work and check whether your actions currently reflect your intended outcome; maybe you'd take up some extra responsibilities at work to look better or put in some more hours. Show your employer that you're worthy of that pay rise.

I have had magical workings been successful without having to do much action, but as a rule of thumb, the most effective magics are the ones where you're putting in the effort, both spiritually, mentally and physically (mind, body and spirit). It is important to remember that the mundane can be magical too, and you can see it like this; how everything that you do to be productive towards your magical goals is magical. Even if it's simply sending off your resumes after performing a job spell or repeating positive affirmations in the mirror after doing a self-love spell. It's all magic and it all feeds into your spellwork. It is worth preplanning this part, as you don't want to find yourself having performed the spell and scrambling to find something to do to get the magic going.

And you're ready to cast! You have crafted your spell and are now prepared to do the magic. If you're newer to casting spells, I encourage you to follow these steps more closely as it'll help you wrap your head around the context for each spell component. The reality is that as you become more experienced with the practice of magic, there is little need for analysing every single part of your spell in long detail, as it just becomes second nature, you develop a sort of spell muscle memory. There will also be moments where you don't have the time or capacity to go through this structure and just need the spell done as soon as possible, and there's no shame in that. You can stress yourself out by looking at every little detail of your spell in the crafting process, and it's easy to become rather excessive with it.

All in all, you can think of crafting your spell like layering up lots of symbology together. Symbolism is a huge part of the occult and always has been. Our brain is hardwired to make sense of the world through symbols, metaphors, imagery and such. The aesthetic aspect of the craft is something which can trap people into solely focusing on, though understanding the meaning behind what we do and why we are doing it is what helps you grow not just your magic, but you as a person. It helps you connect to, what people call, your "higher self".

Chapter 6

The Spellwork Process

All of the research, reading and studying in the world cannot teach you what magic actually is. The study of magic and the occult can last a lifetime, and magic is an experience. After all, it is called magical practice for a reason. The praxis is vital, and now is the time to put what we've learnt to the test.

To give a bit of advice before we detail into the methodology of casting spells, try not to be too disheartened if your first spell does not work or turn out the way you wanted it to be. Many have defined magic as a science for a reason, a lot of is trial and error; testing out different styles and methods until you find one that sticks. A magical path is one to be walked down, not sprinted down towards the end, because ultimately, there isn't really a clear finish line. When somebody first picks up a guitar, they're more than likely not going to be able to play an amazing tune straight away. You have to go back, learn the theory, the chords, different plucking/strumming techniques. Even then, the mastered guitar player still has room to learn more. So, my advice is to enjoy the beautiful, if a little chaotic, spellwork process.

Step One – Cleanse

Before we begin to make the magic happen, it's worth making sure we have a "blank slate", not just internally, but externally too. Using whichever methods suit you best, cleanse yourself, your working space and magical tools you'll be using. We want to go forward in this cleansing process with the intention to clear away any unwanted, disruptive or lingering energy and spirits that will negatively interfere with the spell. This may look like lighting an incense stick and wafting about the smoke around our body, altar and such, until you feel refreshed and ready. It could also entail sprinkling or flicking sacred water whilst repeating an incantation or visualising a bright light stemming from the sky and covering every part of your body and altar/tools.

Sometimes it's not always necessary to cleanse, particularly if you are repeating a spell and want to carry over the same energies or spirits attached to it. More often the case, you won't always have the time to perform a whole cleansing ritual for each individual spell you perform. Especially if it's one you're performing on a whim. But generally speaking, cleansing is an important part of the process as it makes sure we are stepping into the magic making with every chance of success.

Step Two – Centre

After making sure we haven't got any nastiness getting in the way of our magic, we should now be better focused and ready for the task at hand. Regardless if not, we can go on to centre ourselves so that we are further in the right headspace. Magic can be quite draining, especially if you are new to practicing. Many feel this after meditation, where you can become fatigued (mentally, spiritually, or even physically). Powering magic is a heavy process, so taking steps to ensuring we are in the right frame of mind and taking care of our wellbeing is essential a lot of the time.

Choose a method which helps you centre best (see Chapter 2 for advice on ways to centre oneself), but the simplest on-the-go centring method is to bring attention to yourself. Focus on every part of your body, and its place within your surroundings. Take time to be mindful of your breath and count down from ten. You should feel focused and calm. Whenever you're ready, we can move onto the magic.

(Optional) Step Three – Casting a Circle

An additional step that many magical practitioners like to employ in their spellwork is the casting of a protective magical circle. The idea is that when we cast a circle, we are protecting ourselves and our magic from outside influences. As well as this, having a circle set up means that the magic is building up in an enclosed area, ready to be sent out towards our desired goal. It helps towards collating that energy and focusing in on the magic in a concentrated area.

We may require extra protection during our magical practices because when we begin to perform magic, connect with spirits or manipulate energy, it acts like a beacon towards all things spiritual. For example, the more with engage with spirit, the more other spirits (sometimes harmless, sometimes not) notice us. When we are utilising energy more and paying more attention to it, also will we notice the disruptive and 'negative' energy affecting us. Due to these factors, many advise to cast a protective circle before you perform your spell to keep you and the magic contained and safe. Though in reality, it is completely optional. It is certainly a useful skill to know and have under your magical toolbelt, but it is not required to cast an effective spell.

In folk witchcraft, rather than casting a circle, many prefer to incorporate protective sigils or amulets in their practice or petition to spirits (such as familiars) to grant them protection and look out for them. If you want to employ more extra measures in a circle-casting fashion, you can use a magical powder blend or string of magical knots, for example, and form a physical ring around your body and/or altar. You can pair this with a particular chant for the extra effect. As usual, it is down to you what your spellwork process is like, but it may be prudent to at least understand different techniques of circle casting.

How you'd cast a circle can be very tradition-dependent, but there are some go-to methods that many magical practitioners employ as they are quite commonly shared amongst the broader pagan and witchcraft community. "Calling the Quarters" is a widely used method for circle casting, which was popularised by Wicca (derived from the Hermetic Order of the Golden Dawn) and essentially involves facing each cardinal direction (north, east, south, west) and invoking the spirits associated with those directions with certain chants. Which spirits invoked can vary, for example, many Wiccans and non-descript neopagan spaces call upon the "Guardians of the Watchtowers" and their associated elemental correspondences. Going even further, many practitioners vary on the associations for each cardinal direction. In Western Esotericism and Traditional Wicca, we see North being associated with Earth, East with Air, South with Fire and West with Water. However, many don't feel as though they relate to these pairings. Gemma Gary in her works on Cornish and Devonshire focused Traditional Witchcraft poses an alternative set where North is Air, East is Fire, South is Earth and West is Water.[1] The correspondences here can be seen as being more attuned more to the natural world, the Sun rising in the East and therefore attributed to that cardinal direction and the Earth being below us and thus more fitting for South, for example. Go with what associations and symbology makes most sense for you, as it will enforce your connection with spirit or energy and only help your magic more.

In a similar fashion to Calling the Quarters, Traditional Witchcraft paths often use the method of "Laying the Compass". Ian Chambers in his work on *The Witch Compass* outlines that functionally this method of circle casting is different than the aforementioned magic circle, as the compass is not intended to contain or protect energy raised in ritual, but rather is "a system of mapping, journeying, and envisioning the otherworld".[2] However, many traditional witches still employ the compass ritual as a protective measure and a way of capturing magic in an area. There are similarities whereby the practitioner calls to the respective cardinal spirit and/or its elemental association, but further can include differing tools, such as the inclusion of a stang and often the use of substances to line a physical circle. Kelden in his work *The Crooked Path* details laying three rings of wine, ash and salt, whereas Ian Chambers recommends a simple ring of either flour, ash or a white powder. Whilst salt is indeed a highly potent protective magical substance, please avoid pouring it directly onto the earth as it can be very corrosive and damages the soil quality and plant life.

Step Four – Crafting

Here is the fun part – craft the spell! Very little set advice can be given here, as it will be entirely dependent on what your spell has been planned like. Remember the crafting steps:

- What is the goal of your spell and therefore, what type of magic are you going to perform?
- What ingredients are you including in your spell and thus, what correspondences have you included?
- What do you want the spell to look like? When and how are you going to assemble it all together in line with your spell intention and correspondending symbology?
- How are you going to "power" your spell and what charging method are you going to employ?
- Are you going to seal the spell with a particular incantation or physical action?
- What behaviour and actions are you going to employ after casting that aligns with your spell intention?

Overall, make sure to keep your spell goal in mind, maintain that meditative focus and every now and then, take some deep intention breaths. If you get distracted, don't linger on it or mentally punish yourself, just refocus and move forward.

Step Five – Ground and Centre

Usually, after performing a spell, the practitioner tends to ground and centre themselves. You can see this as a common practice in Traditional Wiccan circles, where coven members will have cakes and ale after ritual. This is done because not only can magic can be quite tiring, but also during spells and rituals, we are often entering meditative and trance-like states. They can leave us feeling rather floaty, and it is important to "come down" from them and get back to the physical world. Especially if you are set carry out more attention-heavy tasks soon after, such as driving. So, taking some time to ground and centre is worth doing so that you are safe to go about your day afterwards.

If you find some easy to-go methods of grounding and centring, you can employ these after each spell. It can be as simple as eating some food, sipping a hot drink or listing objects in your surroundings.

The reality is that as you become more of an experienced practitioner, these steps do not feel as long and drawn out because practicing magic and casting spells becomes second nature. You develop muscle memory with these things, especially if you have a regular magical routine. As well as this, there are magical practices such as folk magic customs which are spells, but don't require long preparation. An example of this which I frequently employ is the simple act of placing a hagstone (stone with a natural hole through it) in liminal spaces or corners of my house for protection. Another practice in my regular routine is applying my perfume whilst chanting a particular incantation. Both are magical practices, yet don't necessitate the use of GIMCA to prove to be successful. We can perform magical actions in our daily spiritual routine as a way of developing our magical path, not every single thing we do has to be a spell or a ritual. I guess a common misconception particularly of witchcraft is that you just practice spells, but there is more to magic than that. Just something to keep in mind as you become more advanced with your magical practice.

Chapter 7

Post-Spell Procedures

As Zora Neale Huston once said, the "belief in magic is older than writing."[1] This can be a very grounding statement for the anxious magical practitioner. It is very easy to obsess with the technicalities and research of magic, the formula and the reasoning, but as established before, what is most important to you as a magical practitioner, is the doing. This may come across as rather counter intuitive considering you're reading a book emphasising the technicalities of magic but understand that reading can only get you so far. Ultimately, you'll never understand magic and the experience of it by studying alone. It is inherently a tool of praxis, one which appears and feels different to everyone.

On that note, yes, magic can feel and be different for each individual, so it's vital to acknowledge that comparison can be poisonous. We are surrounded by internet systems and social structures that are designed to make us compare ourselves to each other, and this, of course, bleeds into the magical and spiritual community. Places like social media are amazing spaces to help us understand how other people practice and to get inspiration or advice on how we can adapt and evolve our own practice, but it's important to remember that posts on social media are simply snapshots of a moment in time. They rarely capture the entire picture, the context or background behind the product, the hard work, the failures, and the less pretty parts of the occult. So, keep this in mind when you are practicing magic and developing your spells, that just because your practice looks different to how other practices look like from a glance, does not mean its inferior or not right. It is alarmingly easy to become obsessed with how others perceive us, to be a perfectionist, and to over-concern yourself with how others practice magic/cast spells and whether you should be doing the same as them. The answer is almost always no.

There are lots of opinions on what it and what isn't, and magic is no exception to the rule. You may find yourself called to a particular tradition, which states how magic works in a specific way and has particular methods that it does not deviate from. This is not wrong, but it is not universal across magical practitioners. Magic is magic, no one tradition is 100% correct, go with the flow that is your own personal flavour and intuition – whether that be based in a particular tradition or not. This is noted here since certain traditions may structure their spells a certain way, which will undoubtedly have an impact on the results of the spell.

The Mundane versus the Magical

A common phenomenon that happens often when a practitioner embarks on their magical journey is an over-indulgence in confirmation bias, often passively. In the context of spirituality, this is essentially where the person will take any sensory information they come across, even if seemingly irrelevant or unrelated, and use it to validate their own beliefs. When used foolhardily, the spell caster may see any random objects or occurrences and immediately apply it as something which is related to the spell just performed, without any critical thinking or introspection. It could be a spiritual sign, or it just could be a coincidence. This is where the concept of synchronicity comes into play.

A concept first introduced by the famous psychoanalyst Carl G. Jung, synchronicity is the phenomenon where certain events occur that are similar or seemingly related to each other in a particular way, that aren't actually related to each other. According to Jung, synchronistic moments are 'meaningful coincidences' or 'acausal connections'.[2] To give an example, part of working with spirits may include utilising divination to communicate and receive signs. You may ask a particular spirit a question multiple times over a period of time and receive the same answer each time – such as receiving the same tarot card in each shuffle and pull. These are individual events that are seemingly related, but since they are done on different days, they are not really related to each other. It is here where a rule of thumb is employed, which can be different to each practitioner. A personal guideline of mine I utilise is a rule of three, spaced apart. If three similar events, or 'coincidences' occur at individual moments in time, then it is considered a spiritual sign. It being a rule thumb, there are, of course, exceptions you may want to consider. If the event is particularly obviously related, for example, the exact change the spell goal aims to influence is achieved, then you can be fairly certain the magic worked.

Part of strengthening your magical practice or developing any religious faith you ascribe to, is being able to decipher a balance between what is a synchronicity moment or simply a mundane set of circumstances. Going further, part of what makes magic *magic* is its sacred-ness. For something to be sacred, it must be set apart from what is considered not sacred. In all honesty, the line between the mundane and magical becomes blurry especially for the animist, where the mundane is considered inherently magical or spiritual. It sounds a little complicated, that everything is magic, but also not everything is magic. This is a path that no one can navigate for you unfortunately, and honestly, I find comfort in that things don't have to "make sense" for it to be real. If you look at magic, it really doesn't make sense, but it works. That's all that matters to me.

You can look at it from multiple ways, but I find that simply because something can be explained by mundane factors, does not necessarily mean that moment can't have any spiritual significance for you. It's important to remember that we humans are constantly assigning meaning and purpose to aspects of our lives. Say people who get tattoos, there's times where people just get them because they like the look of it, whereas some others purposefully get tattoos because of their deeper meaning. We assign this meaning, and just because we are the ones that assign it, does not make it any less powerful or meaningful. I can look at the Sun in the sky each day (well, not directly look at it) and understand that it is a huge ball of hot plasma in space which radiates energy as light. But I can also look to the Sun, feel its warm rays on my face and know that it is Sulis (Brittonic Goddess of the Sun) guiding me. The two are not contradictions necessarily, why should they be? I can also understand I have assigned that spiritual meaning as I worship the said Goddess, but that doesn't make my Gods any less real or my spiritual path any less valid for me.

Sceptics will point the magician or witch to science as something which disproves our magical abilities or spiritual signs, but I (personally) do not believe that just because science exists, that means magic cannot. As briefly touched on before, social science such as psychology has given us explanations for the more peculiar human behaviour; confirmation biases and self-fulfilling prophecies, but there is nuance where these come into play with spirituality. Say I've just petitioned a spirit to aid me with an issue, and henceforth I've kept seeing relevant messages on signposts and billboards along the walk to work I've always done. Maybe those messages were always there and now that I've got that magical goal on the forefront of my mind, I've just noticed them more. Who's to say that actually that is the spirit helping me see what is there and relevant to my petition? Why can they not both be true at the same time? Just because you are a magical practitioner does not mean you do not have a rational mind. It is true that we must remain self-aware and grounded in both the physical and spiritual world, as to not harm oneself. But there is a difference between mental health conditions such as psychosis or delusional thinking and being spiritual. In my eyes, so long as you keep a level head, if you think something is magic, let that be magic for you. Overall, discernment is a skill that every magical practitioner learns, largely through trial and error, and it is something that takes time to figure out. So, just take it one spell at a time.

What to Expect When You Are Expecting

What to expect when you are expecting a magical result is tricky. Judging by the common perceptions of magic and witchcraft, usually people expect something fantastical to happen (and sometimes it does), but you would be surprised at how subtly and strangely magic can appear to us.

There will certainly be times where magic works in ways you won't expect it to. Once I performed a relationship enhancement spell to save a failing relationship, only for us to break up not long after. In retrospect, the spell worked, as it did enhance what was there; just what was there was not very good. This is a good example too of where wording your spell goal is important and can have a real impact (though I have to say in this instance, I'm very happy with the result of that spell). To give another example, I once performed a banishing spell to get rid of an awful person from my life, only for them to apologise to me the next day and then after that, I would never see or hear from them again. At the time of the apology, I thought the spell failed considering they actually contacted me after I wanted them to get out of my life. But now looking back, it worked perfectly, just not how I expected.

Something else to consider is not taking in the signs, I am sure I've missed numerous signs and messages after performing spells, it happens. It doesn't necessarily mean your spell didn't work, and as show in the aforementioned examples, there have been spells where it was not until a little while after the situation,

I realised it had actually worked and I just couldn't see it. This can be particularly common with divination, where you do a future guiding reading, for it to play out how the reading said it would and you not even realise. You can perform spells where something amazing will happen the next day after casting the spell, but you may also encounter spells where it's a long four-to-six-month wait to see any results. Magic works in mysterious ways, so when expecting results, try go forward with an open mind and take it one step at a time.

Exercise 6 – Journalling Your Magic

One way to keep track of your results and work at your skills of discernment is to journal. This does not have to be in a large, fancy, leather-bound tome which you call a Book of Shadows or any other mystical name. It can be if you want but focus more on the act of writing itself. A piece of paper and a pen, a document saved in your computer or whatever is most accessible to you will suffice. Writing in itself is a very spiritual process, transforming your thoughts and experiences into a physical form; it's a very powerful and magical thing.

It may be worth writing down any noteworthy spell you perform and what you did, so that after you cast it, you can jot down any experiences you think may or may not be involved with or caused by the magic. Keep your mind open, what you write can be something really small that you think has a little chance of being related to the spell, or even the really obvious results.

I believe that by keeping track of your spells in this methodical way, it allows the practitioner to look back and reflect on their journey, you are able to see directly what went wrong, to notice patterns of why it did and to use this information to improve your future magic.

Before casting the spell, perhaps jot down the following:

- How long before you expect to see results from the spell?
- How many people are involved in the situation and what are their names?
- What type of result do you expect; positive, negative, any particular emotions from any particular parties?
- If the spell does fail or not work out well, do you have any other spells or practices to employ to add to the magic?

After the spell and as time passes, you may want to consider the following journalling prompts to consider engaging your magical thinking:

- How have you felt since casting the spell?
- Has the target (you or someone else) been acting differently that can't be explained by other normal means?
- Have there been any new recurring thoughts related to the spell since you casted it?
- Have you been noticing any repeating symbols, words, sentences around you that can't be explained by common circumstances?
- Do you recall any noteworthy dreams that may be related to the spell?

A practice worth employing at this stage too is divination. Divination is the art of divining the future, of seeking answers from the spirit world and using spiritual means to practice introspection. Where you've casted a spell and are expecting to see some results, perform some divination. Whether you are asking a spirit, the universe, or something/someone else entirely, divine about your spell and journal these results.

How to Dispose of the Spell

This is the most overlooked part of spellcrafting and spellcasting and arguably, one of the most important things to pre-plan.

Disposing of your spell can be very easy and harmless, so try not to overthink it.

More often than not, I see a lot of practitioners advise that the spell must be disposed of in a way which is truly antithetical to the nature worship they claim to practice. This can include throwing spell jars into bodies of water, burying non-biodegradable items in soil (at crossroads, for example), or even flushing waste material such as candle wax down the loo. None of these actions are necessary to conclude a spell, I promise. These practices are a part of many traditions, of which I'd never want to disrespect, however, I believe we can all adapt our magic to be as environmentally friendly as possible, given the decline of our natural spaces, plastic and waste pollution, loss of biodiversity, climate change and other worrying problems our world is facing.

Here is a short list of eco-friendly disposal guidance on common spell items and ingredients:

- Used up dry plant material such as herbs can be burnt (granted they are safe to burn) instead of being buried or thrown in nature. Remember it is illegal in some places to plant non-native invasive species in the wild, so it's best to avoid burying anything out in nature that you are unsure of.
- As well as dry plant material, leaving used food (perhaps given as offerings, for example) out in the wild can have potentially harmful effects. Wildlife will eat scraps of human food left outside, and some animals won't be able to decipher between what is a bit of food in a random location, or somewhere which provides a steady source of food. You can see how this can get problematic with food thrown out of cars, left on the side of the road; animals quickly become roadkill. Be cautious with where

you leave your used offerings or spell ingredients, just because its natural, doesn't mean there won't be any potential negative impacts; nature is not a monolith.

- Leftover candle wax can be reused and made into new candles. Simply heat your wax in a double boiler until it melts, pour it carefully in a heat-proof container and add a wick. There are countless video tutorials online that show step by step how to make different types of candles at home, so it's worth doing some searching.
- Instead of burying your spell jars out in nature which disrupts soil ecosystems, and the glass will virtually never decompose, instead bury it in a plant pot filled with soil in your home or garden. Always avoid burying plastics as they can leech harmful chemicals into the soil and disrupt plant growth.[3]
- Re-use your spell jars and bags. You can purify these items with methods outlined in Chapter 4, mundanely clean them and they are perfectly fine to re-use in your next spell.

Unfortunately, there are lots of other environmentally harmful spiritual practices that are commonly practiced to this day. The placement of coins in trees which causes the tree to die, the over usage of sacred plants such as White Sage (*Salvia apiana*) causing overharvesting and species population decline,[4] the use of salt on the earth to create a magical circle, just to name a few. It can be difficult to know what is harmful for the environment and what isn't, so if you're ever in doubt, it's always worth asking other practitioners. The bottom line is just to think critically on the consequences of your actions, simply because a spell written in a book tells you to throw a jar into a river, doesn't mean you have to, or should.

Chapter 8

Spells

It wouldn't be a book on spells if I didn't include any actual spells, so here are some examples of magical workings that you can try out. These spells are designed using various methods of charging and spiritual means, as to appeal to a wider audience. Don't be afraid to adjust the spells intuitively to your own personal flavour. It is your magical path, after all.

Evil Eye Jewellery Ward Spell

A phenomenon that is found in almost every culture is the concept of the evil eye, the idea of a malicious gaze upon you from somebody that can send harm your way or bring about ill luck. There are thousands of customs for warding off the evil eye, with many being familiar with the eye shaped blue Nazar amulet from Turkey. However, it is quite simply to create your own ward against the evil eye, with this example including very simple knot magic.

This spell is designed to be a ward worn as a jewellery piece. Something which can blend very easily into everyday wear and be perfect against guarding any malicious or accidental ill intent sent your way by anyone. Sometimes the best magic is the ones left unnoticed.

Ingredients:

- A bundle of red string – red is a strong colour of protection and warding against evil in many cultures.
- A bundle of black string – black is also another protective colour in magic.

- ◦ You will want enough string so that it measures around your desired location well, such as your wrist if you're choosing a bracelet, your neck a necklace, or ankle an anklet, etc.

Method:

1. To coincide the spell with the correspondence of protection, its best to perform this spell on a Saturday (Saturn's day), or on a New Moon to symbolise banishing/ repelling negativity.
2. Lay out the ingredients in front of you at your working space.
3. Cleanse yourself, the string and pendant (if applicable) with your preferred cleansing method.
4. Centre your being with your preferred method, until you feel refreshed and ready.
5. Start by creating a twisted rope with the strings.
   a. Details on how to do this can be found on a video on my YouTube channel[1] or, simply add another string (another protective colour or one to your liking) and make a simple plait.
6. Take your cord in your hands and close your eyes. Take some deep, intentional breaths.
7. Visualise a defensive ward surrounding your body.
   a. This can look or feel different for everyone, such as one may enjoy visualisations of bramble surrounding them, or mirrors reflecting harm.
8. Keep these visualisations in mind as you tie nine knots, and as you make each knot, speak the following charm:

By knot of one, the spells begun.
By knot of two, the magic comes true.
By knot of three, so shall it be.

By knot of four, this power is stored.
By knot of five, my will shall drive.
By knot of six, the spell I fix.
By knot of seven, the future I leaven.
By knot of eight, my will be fate.
By knot of nine, what's done is mine.[2]

9. As you tie the last knot, focus all your energy and push it into this knot.
10. Wear the cord to your liking, as a bracelet or anklet, etc.
11. There is minimal action here that you'll do that deviates from your day-to-day behaviour, as you'd want to continue implementing mundane safety measures you always do to protect yourself from harm.

Often, it is said that when a ward breaks, or in this case, maybe if it comes loose or falls off (granted care was undertaken for it to be secured well in the first place), it signifies that it has worked and protected you from a particularly nasty bout of evil eye. If this is the case for you after you conduct the spell, thank the cord for its work and dispose of it appropriately. This can be simply recycling it if possible or throwing it in the bin.

Find Me a Better Job Spell

Are you financially unsatisfied with your current job and are looking to find a different job that pays better? Well let's sort that out with a bit of help from some prosperity magic.

Ingredients:

- A bowl, preferably coloured gold or green to symbolise success and wealth.
- Enough soil to quarter fill your bowl.

- A few handfuls of dried Basil (*Ocimum basilicum*), which has associations with prosperity.
- Loose coins or notes, to symbolise money (literally).

Method:

1. To maximise its efficiency, perform the spell on a Waxing moon, or on a Thursday. Even better if you perform the spell during the hour of Jupiter on a Thursday, invoking that planetary energy before the working.
2. Lay out the ingredients in front of you at your working space.
3. Cleanse yourself, the bowl and money with your preferred cleansing method.
4. Centre your being with your preferred method, until you feel refreshed and ready.
5. Grab the bowl and place it central in your space, start by putting in some soil.
   a. This is symbolic of laying down the foundations to plant the seed of your goal. Reflect on this as you place the soil inside the bowl.
6. Take some basil in your hand, smell its scent and speak to it, "spirit of Basil, I call to thee, shower me in prosperity. Help me achieve my dream, where I receive a job offer that pays an [x]% increase in salary". Say please and thank you as you pour the basil into the bowl, on top of the soil.
   a. Adjust the latter half of the last sentence to your specific desire in your new job.
7. Connect to the energy of the basil, by holding some in your palm, closing your eyes and meditating with the herb. Feel that energy build up and pour it into the bowl.
8. Place the chosen token in the centre of the bowl and bury it partially in the soil.
   a. This is symbolic of planting the seed of your goal.

9. Grab your loose change and place them in the bowl, visualising job offers flooding your email inbox or the company calling you with good news. Focus in on that feeling of success, happiness and excitement.
   a. This is symbolic of watering your seed, giving it nutrients to grow.
10. To seal the spell, repeat those visualisations and hold your hands over the bowl. Meditate on your goal, focus clearly on what you desire and achieving that desire. State clearly your goal and seal the spell: "I receive a job offer that pays an [x]% increase in salary. So mote it be!"
11. Place the bowl in an appropriate location, perhaps on a work desk or by your main computer where you apply for jobs.
12. Act – refresh your resume and send out those job applications.

Once the spell is finished (i.e., you got a new job or have no longer need for the spell), take the loose change out of the bowl. You can dispose of the used basil and soil by composting it, placing it in your food bin, burying in your garden (not in any wild spaces) or simply putting it in the rubbish bin. Clean and purify the bowl and money to be re-used as necessary.

I Am Beauty Self-Love Spell

Love spells are commonly associated with more romantic tropes; tricking crushes into liking you back, stopping lovers from leaving, but love is so much more than this. Love is love, its platonic, familial, romantic, sexual, and most importantly, personal. That cliché is true – you can't love others until you love yourself, and loving ourself is often the hardest thing to do for many of us. Learning to love ourselves is more than just casting a spell, it's a journey through self-expression, contentment, dealing with trauma, and unpacking the darkest parts of ourselves that we hide away. It's hard, and it's a slow process, but its massively rewarding. Self-love is not just making bubble baths and pampering ourselves (though it can be a part of it), it's real, practical work. Whilst practicing self-love goes beyond casting a spell, magic alongside our real work can help the process if it's something you struggle with.

Ingredients:

- A glass jar with a sealable lid.
- String or cord, preferably pink to correspond with love.
- A handful of dried Rose (*Rosa* spp.) petals, for self-love.
- A handful of dried Lavender (*Lavandula* spp.), for happiness.
- You'll only want enough of the prior two ingredients to part-fill the jar as there needs to be space at the top.
- Something to write on that will fit underneath the jar. For example, a piece of paper and a pen, or chalk and a chalkboard, or a wipeable pen and stone surface.

Method:

1. Perform the spell on a Friday, during the hour of Venus, so that you're aligning your spell with correspondences of love.
2. Lay out the ingredients in front of you at your working space.
3. Cleanse yourself, the cord and the glass jar with your preferred cleansing method.
4. Centre your being with your preferred method, until you feel refreshed and ready.
5. On your chosen surface, draw out the kamea/magical square of Venus (of which if unknown, can be found via a quick Google search). If unable to draw, simply draw

out a personal sigil of self-love, or just a love heart if all else fails.

6. Over the drawn-out symbol, grab your jar. Place the rose petals in your hand and speak to the spirit of the rose, "I call to thee rose, help me realise my beauty" and pour it in the jar.

7. Place the lavender in your hand and speak to the spirit of the plant, "I call to thee Lavender, help me find my happiness" and pour it in the jar.

8. Place the jar in the centre of the symbol and place your hands over the mouth, chant: "I am me, I am beauty, I deserve to love myself completely." Repeat this, whilst visualising warm light surrounding yourself.

9. Once content, close the lid of the jar and grab your cord. Wrap it round the neck of the jar and as you tie a knot, seal the spell with "I wind, I bind, this spell be mine!"

10. Shake the jar whenever you need a boost in spirits, repeating the incantation "I am me, I am beauty, I deserve to love myself completely".

11. Take action as well and dedicate some time in your weekly routine to just yourself if you can. This could include some quiet self-reflective meditation or journalling, or perhaps take a solo nature walk. Other self-care procedures such as going to therapy or reaching out to loved ones are also perfect for this spell. Otherwise, maybe perform some of your hobbies with the only goal in mind to just enjoy spending time with yourself.

12. Check in with yourself in a few months' time, reflecting on your progress with your self-love.

This spell doesn't always have an end date, but if you find yourself ready to dispose of this particular spell, then you can do so by removing the natural ingredients inside the jar. Dried lavender and rose are safe to burn, however, be careful with buying store-bought flowers and burning those, as they are often sprayed with harmful chemicals. If your herbs are fine to burn, then you can do so by placing them on a charcoal incense disc or chucking them in a fire. If these are not available options for you, you could compost them or simply put them in your waste bin. Burying the plant material is an option but be sure to only bury it in your own garden or private areas, and not out in the wild. The string can be re-used or thrown away if desired, and the jar can be cleaned and purified, ready for the next spell.

Healing from Afar Spell

In this day and age, most of us have loved ones who are afar, and we cannot always be there physically to help them heal. Spells are fantastic for this; just a little bit of magic to boost the healing process.

For this spell you will need some personal information of your target individual as per the law of contagion for a taglock, their full name and date of birth or even better, personal material of theirs such as hair or nail clippings. However, granted that this is a distance healing spell, it is presumed that you will only have the former which works just as well. The spell intention for this working will, of course, depend on what your suffering individual is dealing with, so always personalise your spell to the situation at hand.

Ingredients:

- White candle of any desired size, white for healing and purification.
- Fire-safe candle holder.
- Lighter or matches.
- Carving tool.
- Three sprigs of Yarrow (*Achillea millefolium*), for healing.
- Taglock of your target.

Method:

1. Conduct the spell on a Thursday, which is associated with health, in the hour of Mercury, symbolising quickness and communication.
2. Lay out the ingredients in front of you at your working space.
3. Cleanse yourself, the candle and the candle holder with your preferred cleansing method.
4. Centre your being with your preferred method, until you feel refreshed and ready.
5. Take your candle and tap it, to "wake" it up.
6. Visualise the person who needs some healing clearly or speak their name out loud nice and clear.
7. Whilst doing so, take your carving tool and carve the targets name into the candle, depending on the size of the candle, spiralling downwards.
8. Once carved, place your candle in your candle holder.
9. Take your Yarrow and connect with it;
   a. Feel its healing energy and let it connect with your own, building up ready to transfer to the candle.
   b. Speak to the Yarrow, asking for its help healing your individual with their specific condition.
10. Place the Yarrow around the candle (be careful with placing it too close to the flame, so it does not catch on fire and cause a hazard).
11. Grab your lighter/matches and make a flame, as you light the candle, continue your visualisations, repeating your spell intention clearly.
12. Lighting the flame is sealing the spell into action here.
13. Depending on the condition that needs healing, let your candle burn.
   a. All the way down in one sitting if a speedy recovery is necessary, or

b. In increments if the healing process will be slow and drawn out over a longer period of time.

14. Make sure your target is taking care of themselves and check in on their mental wellbeing too.

When finished, if candle wax remains, save it to re-use the wax for another candle. If candle making is not your special interest, then simply dispose of it in the bin if this is the most environmentally friendly way you can. The used Yarrow can be disposed of dependent on your location. Here in the UK, Yarrow is a native wildflower, so placing the Yarrow remains in the wild is not an environmental concern.

A note of importance here with healing and general blessing spells, it isn't necessarily about fixating on the result of the magic working or not. Think of it akin to saying good luck to somebody before they take a test. If they pass, the credit is not necessarily yours. This is part of the practice of discernment as discussed prior, but I thought it prudent to mention here as how a body heals depends on a variety of factors that can be out of magic's control. Essentially, don't overthink the results as you might other, more personal, spells.

Safe Travels Spell

This spell is designed for those who travel day-to-day, perhaps to work or any other adventures. It's written with driving to your destination with a car in mind, however, it's not exclusive to this method of transport, of course.

Ingredients:

- Pinch of Mugwort (*Artemisia vulgaris).*
- Black pouch or charm bag.
- Paper and pen.

Method:

1. Perform the spell on a Saturday, the day for Saturn and protection. Pair this with the hour of Mercury, for travel.
2. Lay out the ingredients in front of you at your working space.
3. Cleanse yourself, the charm bag and paper/pen (if necessary) with your preferred cleansing method.
4. Centre your being with your preferred method, until you feel refreshed and ready.
5. Take the Mugwort in your hands and speak to it, feel its energy and spirit and ask it clearly: "Spirit of Mugwort, I call to thee, protect me and my body from harm whilst I travel."
6. As your placing the Mugwort in your charm bag, visualise a reinforced shield around your body (and/or your car, your bicycle, etc.).
7. Grab your paper and tear it small enough so that it will fit in your charm bag.
8. Draw the following on the paper:

EC

TECT

OTECTI

ROTECTIO

PROTECTION

    a. This charm is an adaptation of an ancient charm, whereby the original decaying text is "abracadabra". The staggered addition of letters taps into the idea of sympathetic magic, symbolising the idea of increasing protection.

9. Place this in your charm bag whilst chanting: "Myself and my body are protected wherever I travel and wherever I go,"

10. As you tie your bag seal your spell with "This spell is done, as I say it so."
11. Keep this charm bag close, in your pocket, in the bag you use every day, or if you are casting the spell with a specific mode of transport in mind, such as a car, you could hang it from your rear-view mirror, for example.

You can keep this spell running as long as you may require protection on your travels, as it's designed to be a more long-term spell. When you feel as though the work is done, you can simply take apart the charm bag, dispose of the Mugwort and paper through the appropriate and most environmentally friendly disposal method available to you and save the charm bag for a future spell. Mugwort is a safe to burn herb but be cautious that burning the herb (for example, when smoked) can exhibit very mild psychoactive effects.

Conclusion

We've come to the end of our journey together, but I hope that your path into spellwork continues on. This book doesn't claim to be an all-encompassing manual, rather a guide to foundations of magic through spellwork; an analysis into the bones of spells, how they work and how you can look to craft your own in a more efficient way. The practice of magic is vast, layered and complicated, and there's a reason there are hundreds of thousands of books on magic nowadays. The absence of any particular tradition or magical concept is not done arbitrarily, rather due to lack of time and space in this tome (any writer would say the same).

All in all, understanding how to cast a spell and developing your spells so that they are efficient can feel daunting, but remember spells are fun! What hasn't been touched on is the feeling of burnout, which many practitioners often experience, regularly. You are not alone, it's completely normal. There is so much to learn and experience in the world of magic and spells, no doubt we can get overwhelmed and need to take a break every now and then. Go at your own pace, only you know your own limits and what you can handle. But don't let those fears or assumptions of how you *should* be practicing get you down. Ground yourself in your own world, focus on what is around you, because the magic is already there, at your fingertips, ready to be explored. You need not worry about having an entire library of occult texts or every crystal on the planet, or the perfect practice that pleases everyone. You are ready grow right now. Magic is beautiful and powerful, and so are you.

About the Author

Ariana Carrasca is an English folk witch and Brittonic polytheist from East Anglia in the UK. She was raised into the craft by her mother who is a 3rd Degree Gardnerian Wiccan.

Having been on a magical path for over a decade, she began making educational witchcraft and paganism content on YouTube under the name *The Oak Witch*, aiming to help not just beginners, but any magical practitioners at any stage in their journey.

Outside of the magical world, she has a career in ecology, and is passionate about educating for a more environmentally friendly and eco-conscious magical world.

Notes

Chapter 1

1. Ronald Hutton, *The Stations of the Sun: A History of the Ritual Year in Britain* (Oxford: Oxford University Press, 2001), p4.

2. Edward Burnett Tylor, *Primitive Culture: Researches into the Development of Mythology, Philosophy, Religion, Art, and Custom, Volume 1* (London: John Murray, 1920 [1871]), p417.

3. Engels, David and Nice, Alex. "Divination in Antiquity" in *Prognostication in the Medieval World: A Handbook* edited by Matthias Heiduk, Klaus Herbers and Hans-Christian Lehner, pp15–54. Berlin, Boston: De Gruyter, 2021. https://doi.org/10.1515/9783110499773-001

4. Owen Davies, *Grimoires: A History of Magical Books* (Oxford: Oxford University Press, 2010), p8.

5. Owen Davies, *Popular Magic: Cunning-folk in English History* (London: Hambledon Continuum, 2003), pp119–145.

6. Doreen Valiente, *The Rebirth of Witchcraft* (London: Robert Hale, 1989), p51.

7. Ronald Hutton, *The Triumph of the Moon: A History of Modern Pagan Witchcraft* (Oxford: Oxford University Press, 1999), p214.

8. This claim can be perhaps traced back to a footnote of an edited version of Aleister Crowley's *Liber Aba, Book 4, Part 2* (ed. Mary Desti and Leila Wadde): "The old spelling MAGICK has been adopted throughout in order to distinguish the Science of the Magi from all its counterfeits."

9. Aleister Crowley, "Book Four: Magick in Theory and Practice" in *Magick*, ed. John Symonds and Kenneth Grant (Maine: Samuel Weiser, 1973), p130.

Chapter 2

1. "Aleister Crowley on Record", *British Library*, accessed 9 July 2023, https://blogs.bl.uk/english-and-drama/2014/07/ aleister-crowley-on-record.html - This is a quote taken from an article headline written by John Bull in 1923 about Crowley and it subsequently caught on during the, then, anti-Crowley agenda. One cannot deny the influence Crowley has had on modern esoterica and the occult, however, himself and his works are certainly not free from criticism.

2. Aleister Crowley, "Book Four: Magick in Theory and Practice" in *Magick*, ed. John Symonds and Kenneth Grant (Maine: Samuel Weiser, 1973), p131.

3. Ibid.

4. Durgadas Allon Duriel, *The Little Work: Magic to Transform Your Everyday Life* (Woodbury: Llewellyn Publications, 2020), p16.

5. Donald Michael Kraig, *Modern Magick: Twelve Lessons in the High Magickal Arts* (Woodbury: Llewellyn Publications, 2010), p59.

6. Jason Miller, *The Elements of Spellcrafting: 21 Keys to Successful Sorcery* (Newburyport: New Page Books, 2017), p21.

7. Harry Josephine Giles, "Altars of Transition" *The Modern Craft: Powerful Voices on Witchcraft Ethics*, ed. Claire Askew and Alice Tarbuck (London: Watkins, 2022), p52.

8. Emanuel Swedenborg, *Heaven and Hell*, trans. J. C. Ager (New York: Swedenborg Foundation, 1900), p73.

Chapter 3

1. It is important to add here that western ceremonial occultism has a rich history, of which much is rooted in appropriation unfortunately. Qabala is an example of this, which is based on the Jewish mystical system of

Kabbalah and is often wrongly separated from these roots. More information on this topic can be read at www.jewitches.com.

2. David Salisbury, *Witchcraft Activism: A Toolkit for Magical Resistance* (Maine: Samuel Weiser, 2019), p190.

3. There is too much complexity to detail the history of the Wheel of the Year in this book, so I'll point you to my YouTube video on this topic, of which you can find at: https://www.youtube.com/watch?v=HhsqYuQF9Lw

4. Due to the high demand for crystals in the spirituality and wellness market, problematic aspects of the mining industry have been highlighted and if anything, worsened. From the concept of conflict minerals, poor working conditions for miners, unfair wages, child and slave labour, environmental decimation and more. Watch "The Harm of Healing Crystals" on YouTube for more discussion and resources on this: https://youtu.be/PNYBQVgC75A

5. Doreen Virtue is an author who was known for writing an abundance of books on new age spirituality, however, she has since denounced them. This is brought up not to slander her, but to give context to the origination of the popular usage of angel numbers, which doesn't hold as many ancient ties as people think.

Chapter 4

1. "Sama-vritti (square wave pattern) Pranayama", Yoga with Subhash, accessed 29 January 2023, https://yogawithsubhash.com/2017/06/01/sama-vritti-square-wave-pattern-pranayama/

2. "What is bioenergetics? The Work of Alexander Lowen", Miray Kayacan, Innercamp, accessed 29 January 2023, https://innercamp.com/what-is-bioenergetics-the-work-of-alexander-lowen/

3. Einat Shuper Engelhard, Michal Pitluk, and Michael Elboim-Gabyzon, "Grounding the Connection Between

Psyche and Soma: Creating a Reliable Observation Tool for Grounding Assessment in an Adult Population", *Frontiers in Psychology* 12 (March 2021). https://doi.org/10.3389/fpsyg.2021.621958

4. "Waterfall – Basic vibratory and grounding exercise", Grounding 101, Institute of Body Psychotherapy, accessed 29 January 2023, https://www.instituteofbodypsychotherapy.com/grounding-101-the-waterfall-exercise/

5. "Centering in Psychology", Centering: Definition, Exercises & Quotes, Berkeley Wellbeing Institute, accessed 29 January 2023, https://www.berkeleywellbeing.com/centering.html

6. A detailed tutorial of the LBRP can be found at this link: https://youtu.be/oyao3JZ-Iv0

7. Have a look at the Wikipedia page titled "Methods of divination", it is a wild ride: https://en.wikipedia.org/wiki/Methods_of_divination

Chapter 5

1. "The Harm of Healing Crystals", The Oak Witch, https://theoakwitch.com/the-harm-of-healing-crystals/

Chapter 6

1. Gemma Gary, *Traditional Witchcraft: A Cornish Book of Ways.* (London: Troy Books, 2019), pp117–121.

2. Ian Chambers, *The Witch Compass: Working the Winds in Traditional Witchcraft* (Woodbury: Llewellyn Publications, 2023), p40.

Chapter 7

1. Zora Neale Hurston, *Mules and Men* (New York: Harper Collins, 2009), p21.

2. Carl G. Jung, *Synchronicity: An Acausal Connecting Principle* (Princeton: Princeton University Press, 1973), p19.

3. Boots, B., Russell, C.W. and Green, D.S., 2019. Effects of microplastics in soil ecosystems: above and below ground. *Environmental science & technology*, 53(19), pp11496–11506.
4. I created a video on my YouTube channel detailing the problem of the use of White Sage, as well as Palo Santo: https://youtu.be/5TVIIE9QW70

Chapter 8

1. To watch the video, follow this link: https://youtu.be/yWQCqOe_ioY?t=519
2. This incantation is a famous charm which, to my knowledge, has blurry origins but is referred to as the "Witches Ladder". The accompanying physical charm is nine knots with trinkets tied in each knot, e.g., feathers.

Recommended Reading

For more recommendations, resources and general magical advice, visit my YouTube channel "The Oak Witch", where I educate on all things magic, witchcraft and paganism. Here I go into more detail about specific recommendations. However, I thought it prudent to leave a list of my recommended books for any magical practitioner looking to improve their craft:

Bringing Race to the Table: Exploring Racism in the Pagan Community **edited by Crystal Blanton, Brandy Williams and Taylor Ellwood** – though catered towards the pagan community, this book is applicable for all of which are magically inclined. The issues discussed in here are relevant for anyone establishing their magical path and navigating different traditions and communities.

Cartomancy in Folk Witchcraft: Divination, Magic and Lore **by Roger J. Horne** – this is a great guide for anyone looking to step into cartomancy using playing cards. Even for those who want to better understand the minor arcana in tarot can benefit from this book.

Consorting with Spirits: Your Guide to Working with Invisible Allies **by Jason Miller** – for anyone who enjoys working the spirit model and wants to improve their spirit communication, with both folk and ceremonial magic perspectives.

Defence Against the Witches' Craft: Anti-cursing Charms from English Folk Magick, Traditional Witchcraft and the Grimoire Traditions **by John Canaard** – an excellent little book on protection magic from the perspective of English folk magic.

Folk Witchcraft: A Guide to the Lore, Land & the Familiar Spirit for the Solitary Practitioner by **Roger J. Horne** – this is a lovely book for any beginner witch who knows they are more folk magic inclined.

Practical Planetary Magick: Working the Magick of the Classical Planets in the Western Mystery Tradition, by **David Rankine and Sorita d'Este** – a great guide to the use of the seven classical planets in magic.

Sacred Earth Celebrations by **Glennie Kindred** – a lovely book on the neopagan wheel of the year.

Six Ways: Approaches & Entries for Practical Magic by **Aidan Wachter** – this is a fantastic guide for any magical practitioner who wants to understand magical basics.

Thirteen Pathways to Occult Herbalism by **Daniel A. Schulke** – a beautiful book on the basics of plant magic.

The Witch's Path: Advancing Your Craft at Every Level by **Thorn Mooney** – a must have for anyone looking to move beyond being a beginner witch (or general magical practitioner)

Witchcraft Activism: A Toolkit for Magical Resistance by **David Salisbury** – this is a good guide to what justice magic is in the context of witchcraft.

Bibliography

Averis, B. (2013) *Plants and Habitats; An Introduction to Common Plants and their Habitats in Britain and Ireland,* Self-published.

Crowley, A. (1997) *Magick: Liber ABA, Book Four, Parts I-IV,* York Beach, Samuel Weiser.

Davies, O. (2003) *Popular Magic: Cunning-folk in English History,* London, Hambledon Continuum.

Davies, O. (2009) *Grimoires: A History of Magic Books,* Oxford, Oxford University Press.

Duriel, D. A. (2020) *The Little Work: Magic to Transform Your Everyday Life,* Woodbury, Llewellyn Publications.

Frazer, J. G. (1890) *The Golden Bough: A Study of Magic and Religion,* London, Macmillan and Co.

Gary, G. (2008) *Traditional Witchcraft: A Cornish Book of Ways,* London, Troy Books.

Giles, H. J. (2022) 'Altars of Transition' in Askew, C. and Tarbuck, A. *The Modern Craft: Powerful Voices on Witchcraft Ethics,* London, Watkins.

Hutton, R. (1996) *The Stations of the Sun: A History of the Ritual Year in Britain,* Oxford, Oxford University Press.

Hutton, R. (1999) *The Triumph of the Moon: A History of Modern Pagan Witchcraft,* Oxford, Oxford University Press.

Kindred, G. (2014) *Sacred Earth Celebrations,* Hampshire, Permanent Publications.

Kraig, D. M. (2010) *Modern Magick: Twelve Lessons in the High Magickal Arts,* Woodbury, Llewellyn Publications.

Miller, J. (2017) *The Elements of Spellcrafting: 21 Keys to Successful Sorcery,* Newburyport, Red Wheel/Weiser.

Rankine, D & d'Este, S. (2007) *Practical Planetary Magick: Working the Magick of the Classical Planets in the Western Mystery Tradition,* London, Avalonia.

Salisbury, D. (2019) *Witchcraft Activism: A Toolkit for Magical Resistance*, Maine, Samuel Weiser.

Swedenborg, E. (1900) *Heaven and Hell* (trans. J. C. Ager), New York, Swedenborg Foundation.

Tylor, E. B. (1871) *Primitive Culture: Researches Into The Development of Mythology, Philosophy, Art and Custom*, London, J. Murray.

U.: D.:, F. (2021) 'Models of Magic in Practice' in U.: D.:, F. *Living Magic: Contemporary Insights and Experiences from Practicing Magicians*, Woodbury, Llewellyn Publications.

Valiente, D. (1989) *The Rebirth of Witchcraft*, Ramsbury, Robert Hale.

MOON BOOKS
PAGANISM & SHAMANISM

What is Paganism? A religion, a spirituallty, an alternativo
belief system, nature worship? You can find support for
all these definitions (and many more) in dictionaries,
encyclopaedias, and text books of religion, but subscribe to
any one and the truth will evade you. Above all Paganism is
a creative pursuit, an encounter with reality, an exploration
of meaning and an expression of the soul. Druids, Heathens,
Wiccans and others, all contribute their insights and literary
riches to the Pagan tradition. Moon Books invites you
to begin or to deepen your own encounter,
right here, right now.

If you have enjoyed this book, why not tell other readers by
posting a review on your preferred book site.

Bestsellers from Moon Books
Pagan Portals Series

The Morrigan
Meeting the Great Queens
Morgan Daimler
Ancient and enigmatic, the Morrigan reaches out to us.
On shadowed wings and in raven's call, meet the ancient Irish
goddess of war, battle, prophecy, death, sovereignty, and magic.
Paperback: 978-1-78279-833-0 ebook: 978-1-78279-834-7

The Awen Alone
Walking the Path of the Solitary Druid
Joanna van der Hoeven
An introductory guide for the solitary Druid, The Awen Alone
will accompany you as you explore, and seek out your
own place within the natural world.
Paperback: 978-1-78279-547-6 ebook: 978-1-78279-546-9

Moon Magic
Rachel Patterson
An introduction to working with the phases of the Moon, what
they are and how to live in harmony with the lunar year and to
utilise all the magical powers it provides.
Paperback: 978-1-78279-281-9 ebook: 978-1-78279-282-6

Hekate
A Devotional
Vivienne Moss
Hekate, Queen of Witches and the Shadow-Lands, haunts the pages
of this devotional bringing magic and enchantment into your lives.
Paperback: 978-1-78535-161-7 ebook: 978-1-78535-162-4

Bestsellers from Moon Books

Keeping Her Keys
An Introduction to Hekate's Modern Witchcraft
Cyndi Brannen
Blending Hekate, witchcraft and personal development
together to create a powerful new magickal perspective.
Paperback: 978-1-78904-075-3 ebook 978-1-78904-076-0

Journey to the Dark Goddess
How to Return to Your Soul
Jane Meredith
Discover the powerful secrets of the Dark Goddess and
transform your depression, grief and pain into healing
and integration.
Paperback: 978-1-84694-677-6 ebook: 978-1-78099-223-5

Shamanic Reiki
Expanded Ways of Working with Universal Life Force Energy
Llyn Roberts, Robert Levy
Shamanism and Reiki are each powerful ways of healing; together,
their power multiplies. Shamanic Reiki introduces techniques to
help healers and Reiki practitioners tap ancient healing wisdom.
Paperback: 978-1-84694-037-8 ebook: 978-1-84694-650-9

Southern Cunning
Folkloric Witchcraft in the American South
Aaron Oberon
Modern witchcraft with a Southern flair, this book is a
journey through the folklore of the American South and
a look at the power these stories hold for modern witches.
Paperback: 978-1-78904-196-5 ebook: 978-1-78904-197-2

Readers of ebooks can buy or view any of these bestsellers by clicking on the live link in the title. Most titles are published in paperback and as an ebook. Paperbacks are available in traditional bookshops. Both print and ebook formats are available online.

Find more titles and sign up to our readers' newsletter
www.collectiveinkbooks.com/paganism

For video content, author interviews and more, please subscribe to our YouTube channel.

MoonBooksPublishing

Follow us on social media for book news, promotions and more:

Facebook: Moon Books

Instagram: @MoonBooksCI

Twitter: @MoonBooksCI

TikTok: @MoonBooksCI